After
the
Rain

AFTER THE RAIN

JOHN BOWEN

Random House · New York

For
Vivian Matalon
and
Alec McCowen

AFTER THE RAIN *was first presented in the United States on October 9, 1967, by Helen Jacobson (by arrangement with John Roberts) at the John Golden Theatre in New York City with the following cast:*

(*In order of appearance*)

LECTURER	Paul Sparer
HIS TWO ASSISTANTS	Edward J. Moore
	Alan Rachins
CAPTAIN HUNTER	Anthony Oliver
ARTHUR HENDERSON	Alec McCowen
GERTRUDE FORBES-COOPER	Nancy Marchand
TONY BATCH	Bill Burns
WESLEY OTTERDALE	John Carpenter
MURIEL OTTERDALE	Maureen Pryor
HAROLD BANNER	Alan MacNaughtan
ALAN ARMITAGE	John Colenback
SONYA BANKS	Gretchen Gorbett

Directed by Vivian Matalon
Scenic designs by Brian Currah
Sets executed by Paul Morrison
Lighting by Tharon Musser
Costumes by Domingo A. Rodriguez

The action takes place in a university lecture hall.
The time is two hundred years after the Rain of 1969.

Act One

The curtain is up. Only a few simple and necessary objects are on what is otherwise a bare stage. There are eight straight chairs against the back wall. There is a lectern to one side, downstage. Also to one side, where the wings would be, are chairs for the two ASSISTANTS, *and a wooden table which has a number of hand props on it—books, the logbook,* CAPTAIN HUNTER's *homemade spear. There are also large white cards in holders. One card is lettered "Hold," one "Cabin," two "Deck," and two "Sea."*

Note on the objects and on costumes: *Two hundred years after the Rain of 1969 a society has grown, founded by the six survivors of our play. (There may have been other societies from other survivors, but we are not concerned with them.) The clothes and furniture of this society will be based on an imperfect tradition of what life was like in 1969, modified by the fact that this society has had to rediscover a large number of skills. Clothes and furniture should not be outrageous or science-fictionish, but they should be different.*

The house lights remain up as the ASSISTANTS *enter and take their places. Then the* LECTURER *enters and arranges his notes on the lectern. When he is ready he speaks.*

LECTURER   Lower the lights, please, Mr. Porter, and take the names of any latecomers. I'll see them in punishment room this evening after discussion. (*The house lights are lowered*) In my first lecture, I tried to give a general review of life before the Rain of 1969. For our reconstruction of that time we have to rely on secondary sources—

that is, on the books actually on board the raft on which our forefathers survived. I myself am not convinced of the value as source books either of *Goldfinger* or *Better Sight without Glasses*. There are many areas of life in 1969 about which we can only speculate. For life on board the raft we have two direct sources. The first is the Book of Arthur, which seems in part to be allegorical. The second is the diary of Alan Armitage. The raft itself was destroyed in the fire of 1998, and we have no picture of it. There seems to have been a central structure consisting of a main saloon, with kitchen and bathroom, a smaller cabin, and a hold beneath. The deck, of which we show you only a part, ran all round this central structure. The raft was not part of any survival scheme. It had been built and launched before the Rain began by the International Unitarian Breakfast Food Company, the makers of Glub, a kind of cereal food. (*He clicks his fingers*) Placards, please. (ASSISTANTS *hold up placards illustrating a packet of Glub Flakes*) Thank you. What you see is a box of Glub Flakes. There were also Glub Grits, Glub Cushions, and Poppity Glub for children. It was the contention of the International Unitarian Breakfast Food Company that man could live by Glub alone. They therefore stocked a raft with it, and employed a man to sail it around the world. Thank you, gentlemen. (*The placards are put away*) That man was Captain Hunter. (HUNTER *enters and takes up a position, stage center*) You are Hunter.

HUNTER   Yes, I'm Hunter.

LECTURER   By?

HUNTER   George. I'm Hunter, by George. Actually.

4

LECTURER   Thank you. How did you get this employment?

HUNTER   I was Regular Army, but they retired me. Everything got so bloody technical, you see. Then I tried out for keeping a pub, but they wouldn't have me. Something to do with IQ—you had to draw patterns upside down and say which words didn't fit. I got a bit depressed, actually. Then I was reading a copy of *The Director* at my dentist's, and there was this ad to sail a raft around the world. Turned out all the other volunteers were nut cases or Norwegians, so they gave it to me.

LECTURER   What happened?

HUNTER   About living on Glub? Well, I did a lot of fishing.

LECTURER   And?

HUNTER   I got lost. Radio conked out. Never knew whether I was coming or going. Natural condition for me, as a matter of fact.

LECTURER   And?

HUNTER   It started raining. Didn't stop. Dead calm, mind, wherever I was, but it just went on raining. Monotonous. Then one night I hit a fishing boat. Swamped it. Nobody in it but Arthur and Gertrude and Tony and a lot of dead chaps.

LECTURER   So?

HUNTER   Arthur took over.

LECTURER   Sit down now. (HUNTER *sits on one of the chairs at the back*) These were Arthur Henderson, Gertrude Forbes-Cooper, and Anthony Batch. (*To* ASSIST-ANT) Henderson, next. (ARTHUR *enters and takes up position*) You may be puzzled by the name "Henderson." Our ancestors used the suffix "son" in names just as we do—Cook*son*, Baker*son*, Master*son*, Farmer*son*—but what a "Hender" was, we've not yet been able to discover. (*To* ARTHUR) You are Arthur Henderson?

ARTHUR (*Slight pause*) Yes.

LECTURER Yes, what?

ARTHUR I am Arthur Henderson.

LECTURER Profession?

ARTHUR Accountant.

LECTURER Vocation?

ARTHUR Leader.

LECTURER Explain.

ARTHUR When the orders came to move to camps on the high ground, I knew what would happen. Cholera. Rioting. Food running out. I took a few who would follow me and set out for myself.

LECTURER You chose badly. Most died.

ARTHUR I took those who would come. Two lived.

LECTURER Yes. (*To* ASSISTANTS) Forbes-Cooper and Batch.

 (GERTRUDE *and* TONY *enter and join* ARTHUR)

ARTHUR I began with two of the most necessary parts of man's nature. Miss Forbes-Cooper represented the Arts. Batch had bodily strength. Intelligence I had myself.

LECTURER You are Gertrude Forbes-Cooper.

GERTRUDE Yes.

LECTURER You are Anthony Batch.

TONY I am Tony Batch.

LECTURER Your life before?

GERTRUDE I taught speech and drama at the Royal Academy of Dramatic Art. Then, as it rained and rained, I became quite isolated. The streets filled with water and the people in the basement tried to move upstairs. No proper arrangements had been made, and I couldn't have those people in my flat. Luckily I met Arthur shortly afterward.

TONY "What do you do?" he says. "I'm a strong man," I says. "Right," he says, "I'll have you."

LECTURER Thank you. Sit down. (GERTRUDE *and* TONY *sit on chairs at the back;* LECTURER *speaks to* ARTHUR) What other people did you pick up when you had reached the raft?

ARTHUR I decided to accept anyone who came, if he were healthy and had some sort of skill. Unfortunately, most of those we found were, by that time, no longer healthy. Consequently, they were left to die.

LECTURER (*To* ASSISTANTS) The Otterdales now, and Banner.

7

ARTHUR   The Otterdales were in reasonable health, however. And Banner was clearly an educated man.
(WESLEY, MURIEL, *and* BANNER *enter and take positions by* ARTHUR)

LECTURER   You are Wesley Otterdale.

WESLEY   Yes.

LECTURER   Muriel Otterdale, his wife.

MURIEL   Yes.

LECTURER   Harold Banner, a priest of the Church in
England.

BANNER   Of. Not "in."

LECTURER   What?

BANNER   Lots of churches *in* England. Just the one, *of.*

LECTURER   Very good. (*To* MURIEL) You came from?

MURIEL   Birmingham. We came in a rowing boat with the
Reverend.

LECTURER   A rowing boat?

BANNER   I rowed number six in the Oxford boat.

MURIEL   Mr. Banner's hands got all blistered, and he rowed
and rowed. He didn't let me take a turn; he was that ob-
stinate. And Wesley wouldn't. He said the Rain was a
punishment, you see, and it was God's will not to row.

LECTURER   Thank you.
(*The three sit down.* ARTHUR *lingers*)

ARTHUR There were two others.

LECTURER I know it. Sit down. (*As* ARTHUR *does so,* LEC-
TURER *speaks to* ASSISTANTS) And I'll have the last two.
(*One* ASSISTANT *goes off.* ALAN *and* SONYA *enter*) You are
Sonya Banks?

SONYA I am Sonya Banks.

LECTURER You are Alan Armitage?

ALAN I am Alan Armitage.

LECTURER Sit. (ASSISTANT *returns, pulling a board on
wheels or rollers, which is to do duty as a rubber dinghy.
It must be possible for three people to sit comfortably on
it. It is left to one side of the "deck" space—as if in the
sea. Meanwhile* ALAN *and* SONYA *sit down.* LECTURER *goes
upstage to the row of chairs*) When I snap my fingers, you
will sleep until I order you to wake. You will sleep and
hear nothing. When I say "Wake," you will wake. Sleep
now. (LECTURER *snaps his fingers. All the performers drop
into sleep, except* ARTHUR, *who remains looking at the
LECTURER*) You will sleep. I will snap my fingers once,
and you will sleep. (*He snaps his fingers. A long pause.
He snaps his fingers again.* ARTHUR'S *head drops in sleep.*
LECTURER *hesitates a moment, obviously worried, then
comes back downstage*) New students may be unfamiliar
with our procedure at these lectures. It is most important
that there should be no distractions from the hall. Consequently I must ask you not to cough, whisper, or indulge
in love-play of any kind. Each of these criminals is under
deep hypnosis to enable him to be the person he presents
to you. Before the Rain, this was called acting, and was
used, as we use it, for educational purposes. If the hyp-

9

nosis should be broken by distraction, the consequences might be unfortunate. Please remember that although these people *are* criminals, that is no reason for you to put them at risk, especially since, when this task is over, they will have earned remission and will be permitted to return to normal community duties. (*He speaks to the characters*) Wake. (*They do so*) Places. (ALAN *and* SONYA *enter the boat.* ARTHUR *takes his chair to the upstairs section and sits.* GERTRUDE, MURIEL, WESLEY, *and* BANNER *take theirs to the main saloon.* HUNTER *puts on a pair of oilskins and goes on deck.* TONY *stays where he is*) Raining. (HUNTER *turns up his collar and reacts to the rain*) Begin.

> (ALAN *and* SONYA *have also reacted to the rain, but more as if they had been in it for a long time, and are used to being soaked.* ALAN *is rowing. An* ASSISTANT *pulls the board perhaps one step forward.* SONYA *is singing in a little thin voice*)

SONYA (*Singing*)
> Cruising down the river,
> On a Sunday afternoon.
> The sun above, and one you love . . .

ALAN   Hush up, love. I can see a light. (*Calls*) Ahoy!
> (ASSISTANT *echoes his call in a much fainter voice, and* HUNTER *reacts to the* ASSISTANT)

ASSISTANT   Ahoy!
> (HUNTER *cocks his head and listens*)

ALAN   Ahoy! Ahoy there!

ASSISTANT (*Fainter*)   Ahoy! Ahoy there!
> (HUNTER *turns and goes into the main cabin, where* BANNER *has opened one of the books on the table*

and is reading. GERTRUDE *seems (in mime) to be knitting some intractable material,* WESLEY *stares straight in front of him, and* MURIEL *watches* WES-LEY. ALAN *continues to row, and* ASSISTANT *takes another couple of steps forward)*

HUNTER Arthur?

BANNER Inside.
(HUNTER *goes to the "upstairs" section and mimes knocking)*

HUNTER Arthur?

ARTHUR Yes?

HUNTER Permission to enter, Arthur?

ARTHUR What is it?

HUNTER A shout. Somebody else must have found us.

ALAN *(Calls)* Ahoy!

ASSISTANT *(Not as faint as before)* Ahoy!

ARTHUR Could you see anything?

HUNTER No, Arthur. The rain . . .

ARTHUR Very well. *(Gets up)* I shall come with you. Do you have your spear?

HUNTER It's in the toilet.

ARTHUR Get it.

HUNTER Aye, aye, Arthur.
(ASSISTANT *comes forward, takes the spear from the*

table, and gives it to HUNTER, *while* ARTHUR *moves into the main cabin)*

ALAN   Ahoy! Ahoy there!

ASSISTANT *(Nearer)*   Ahoy! Ahoy there!

HUNTER   Ready, Arthur?

ARTHUR   Yes. Go first with your spear.
(HUNTER *goes out on deck, followed by* ARTHUR. ASSISTANT *brings the wooden board almost to the edge of the deck space.* ALAN *stops rowing)*

ALAN   Ahoy! Is anyone there?

ARTHUR   Stay where you are.
(ALAN *rows a stroke.* ASSISTANT *moves a little forward)*

ALAN   Can we come aboard?
(ARTHUR *motions* HUNTER *to the edge of the platform.* HUNTER *takes up a position of offense)*

ARTHUR   Stay where you are, I said. If you come any closer, I shall request Captain Hunter to jab you with his spear.

SONYA   Goodness!

ARTHUR   Are you ready, Captain Hunter?

HUNTER   Aye, aye, Arthur.

ARTHUR   Then stand by to repel boarders.

ALAN   Is anything wrong? Can we come aboard?

SONYA   He can't mean it.

ARTHUR   Hunter! (HUNTER *appears about to jab down-ward*) I've warned you. You have only yourselves to blame if you should sustain injury.
(*A pause.* ALAN *looks at* SONYA)

ALAN   Come on, Sonn. We'll be on our way.
(*He makes a turning motion with a mimed paddle.* ASSISTANT *turns the board*)

SONYA (*Wails*)   Oh, please can't we stay!

ALAN   We'll find somewhere else.
(*The board moves a little away*)

HUNTER (*Uncomfortable*)   Er . . . Permission to speak, Arthur?

ARTHUR   Yes.

HUNTER   They do look . . . harmless, you know.

ARTHUR   That is not the question. (*Calls*) You! Boat people! You need not leave us yet. I wish to interrogate you, if you are prepared to suffer it. How old is the woman?
(ALAN *stops rowing*)

ALAN   Twenty-three.

ARTHUR   Is she healthy?

ALAN   She's healthy.

ARTHUR   Who are you? Are you husband and wife?

ALAN   No.   SONYA   Yes.

13

ARTHUR   What?

ALAN   Yes, we are.   SONYA   Not exactly

ARTHUR   It is of no consequence. I suppose we could take the woman anyway. You! What do you *do?*

ALAN   Do?

ARTHUR   For a living.
   (*Pause*)

ALAN   I'm a cook.
   (SONYA *looks at* ALAN *in amazement*)

ARTHUR   Can you cook fish?

ALAN   I can cook anything.

HUNTER   I say, must be all right, then?

ARTHUR   There is nothing to be lost by trying him. He may be able to devise a dish which incorporates your breakfast cereal, Captain Hunter.

HUNTER   Oh, I say!

ARTHUR   You may allow them to board the raft. The dinghy at least may be useful to us. See if you can find some bolt or hook to which it may be secured.

HUNTER   There's a sort of ring thing.

ARTHUR   By all means, let them use the ring thing. Carry on, Captain Hunter.

HUNTER   Aye, aye, Arthur. (ARTHUR *turns, goes into the cabin, and sits. Meanwhile* HUNTER *has extended his spear, butt first, and* ALAN—*with the* ASSISTANT *pulling— has moved the raft close enough for* SONYA *to grasp the butt of the spear. The board is pulled right close to the "deck" cards*) You can come up, then, eh? (SONYA *mimes pulling herself aboard.* HUNTER *puts down his spear to help her*) How do you do.

SONYA   How do you do.
           (ALAN *mimes climbing aboard*)

HUNTER   My name's Hunter.

SONYA   Yes, we heard. (*Looks around*) It's nice here.

HUNTER   Oh . . . Do you think so?

ALAN   My name's Alan Armitage. This is Sonya Banks. Do you want me to tie our dinghy up?

HUNTER   No, I'll do it. The ring thing's a bit difficult to find.

ALAN   Thank you.
           (HUNTER *takes the board to stage right and ties it up;* ASSISTANT *takes the spear from him*)

SONYA   Why did you tell them you were a cook? You're a writer.

ALAN   He wouldn't have let me on board unless I could do something useful.

SONYA   He didn't ask me.

ALAN   What?

SONYA If I could . . . Anything. Just if I was healthy. *Can* you cook?

ALAN I'm not bad. (*Pause*) We can take a chance and go. Find somewhere else. (*Pause*) I'm supposed to protect you.

SONYA You've done all right. (*Pause*) What do you think?

ALAN I think we should stay.
(HUNTER *returns*)

HUNTER Expect you'd like to come in and meet the chaps, eh?

ALAN Yes, we should.

HUNTER Well, it's in here. I'll go first.
(HUNTER *goes into the main-cabin area.* ALAN *starts to follow.* SONYA *touches his arm. He turns, and looks at her. Then he puts his arm around her and they kiss passionately, as if they weren't sure when they'd have the chance again*)

LECTURER Supper. (*They move immediately to their places.* ARTHUR *remains in the cabin.* MURIEL *is serving stew from an imaginary stewpot.* ALAN, SONYA, BANNER, GERTRUDE, HUNTER, *and* WESLEY *take their places at the table, leaving a place for* TONY, *and leaving the head of the table empty for* ARTHUR) Begin.

MURIEL I told Arthur I couldn't cook fish. Wesley doesn't like it—he's never cared for it. I said to Arthur, you can't do what you're not used to in this world, and I've never been used to cooking fish. And he said, being as there was nobody else could cook at all, and being as there was only fish to cook, I'd have to make a start at it, but if we found anyone better, I could leave off. And . . .

HUNTER (*To* ALAN) Now we've found you, eh? Lucky thing really. No offense, Mrs. Otterdale.

ALAN Very lucky.

HUNTER Of course we all have our tasks. Discipline must be maintained, eh? Always things to be done. That's what Arthur says. When I was here on my own, I got a bit slack actually. Wrong. I see that now.

ALAN What sort of things?

BANNER Making nets. Stuffing the cracks in barrels with string.

WESLEY (*Cheerfully, energetically*) The crackling of thorns beneath the pot!
(*He begins to make a droning, humming sound, which continues through the following speeches until* MURIEL *cuts him off*)

HUNTER Fishing. Cooking. Lookout duty.

WESLEY The fool hath said in his heart, there is no God. Corrupt are they and have done abominable iniquity. There is none that doeth good.
(*He drones*)

BANNER Sweeping out the hold. Straightening nails. Making furniture out of old crates.

WESLEY Every one of them is gone back. They are altogether become filthy.
(*He drones*)

17

GERTRUDE   Reading aloud after supper. Discussion groups.

WESLEY (*Rises and shouts*)   The workers of iniquity eat up my people as they eat bread.
(WESLEY *sits*)

MURIEL   Well, I'll go and call him, then. (MURIEL *moves to the cabin area and mimes knocking*) Arthur!

ARTHUR   Just coming.

ALAN   What does he do in there?

BANNER   I believe he thinks a great deal.

ARTHUR   Where is Mr. Batch?

HUNTER   Fishing.

ARTHUR   No matter. We shall start without him. Mr. Banner, please say grace.

BANNER   For what we are about to receive, may the Lord make us truly thankful.

ARTHUR   Amen. (*To them all*) Start.
(*They mime eating*)

ALAN   I'd be a bit more thankful if it were pork chops or a mixed grill.

HUNTER   So should I, by George. Or a whacking great steak.

ARTHUR   That will do. I don't permit irreverence, Mr. Armitage. Not for any superstitious reasons—I am an agnostic myself—but because I find that an element of formality at mealtimes helps to remind us that we are civilized beings. I should have preferred a Latin grace, but unfortunately Mr. Banner failed his degree, and cannot remember any.

BANNER   I am a broad churchman, you know.

ARTHUR   On this raft, Mr. Banner, you will be the sort of churchman *I* decide, and no other. Remember that. (TONY *walks down the deck area, and enters the main cabin*) How large is your catch?

TONY   I only got three.

ARTHUR   You are below your target, then.

TONY   I'm sorry, Arthur.

ARTHUR   You had better meet Mr. Armitage. He is to be our chef from now on. And this is Miss Banks. Mr. Batch is a strong man; Miss Banks is a dancer. I expect you will have much in common.
(TONY *gives a sort of half-nod, half-bow*)

SONYA   A strong man?

TONY   Well, I do exercises. With weights and that.

SONYA   Where?

TONY   Y.M.C.A.
(TONY *goes off into the kitchen*)

SONYA   (*Disappointed*)   Oh. . . I thought there might be a hold somewhere.

ARTHUR   But there is a hold. That is an excellent idea. Do you think you could improvise equipment, Mr. Batch?

TONY   Equipment?

ARTHUR   Weights.

TONY   I could make something. With boxes and bits of chain and that.

ARTHUR   Excellent, excellent.

TONY   Then I'd need a bit of board. For when you lie down on an inclined plane. What they call an inclined plane, in the gym. That's for lying on. And lifting. You lie on it, and then you lift. It strengthens the stomach.

ARTHUR   Captain Hunter, no doubt there are bits of board in the hold?

HUNTER   By George, yes. Lots of bits of board.

TONY   I'd need a bit of board, then, for the inclined plane.

ARTHUR   And you shall have one.
        (TONY *comes to sit down by* SONYA. *It is clear that he regards her as someone who shares his interests*)

SONYA   I thought . . .

ARTHUR   Yes, Miss Banks? What did you think? Have no hesitation in telling me.

SONYA   I thought if Tony was going to practice in the hold, maybe I could too.
        (*Slight pause.* ARTHUR *looks at* SONYA *and* TONY *and gets the beginnings of an idea*)

ALAN (*A little unhappy*) Er . . .

ARTHUR (*Tops him*) By all means, Miss Banks; by all means. Our new society will need every skill, every art. (*Looks from* SONYA *to* TONY) Practice by all means.

LECTURER Wait. (*Characters remain still.* LECTURER *speaks to the audience*) The Book of Arthur is in fact a set of books. It began as the ship's log, and was kept up irregularly by Hunter—there are occasional entries— "Thunder today" or "Trouble with sharks," and a number of asterisks that may have referred, oh, to some solitary sexual practices. Arthur himself began to write up the log on his arrival, but all the early material has been amended, crossed out, and written over. Consequently, for a statement of Arthur's intentions at the beginning of the voyage, the diary of Alan Armitage appears to be a more reliable source. (*To the characters*) Conversation on deck.

> (ALAN *and* ARTHUR *leave their places at the table and begin to pace the deck*)

ARTHUR Tell me, Mr. Armitage, have you come to any explanation in your mind about this flood?

ALAN God, I suppose.

ARTHUR So Mr. Otterdale would say. He believes it to be some form of divine punishment for his own sins. A common delusion.

ALAN Has he sinned much?

ARTHUR Hardly at all.

ALAN Mad?

ARTHUR   One might say so.

ALAN   I'm surprised you keep him.
(*Pause.* ARTHUR *looks sharply at* ALAN)

ARTHUR   His wife is attached to him.

ALAN   And Mr. Banner? Doesn't *he* say God's sent the rain?

ARTHUR   Mr. Banner is a very broad churchman. It is not clear that he believes in God at all.

ALAN   And you?

ARTHUR   I say that it is the best thing that could ever have happened.

ALAN   I don't understand you.

ARTHUR   Natural selection is responsible for this flood, Mr. Armitage, and by natural selection certain people will survive it. I shall be one of them. So will you, as long as you obey me.

ALAN   Why did natural selection pick us, do you think?

ARTHUR   I can see you are not a serious student of human affairs, Mr. Armitage.

ALAN   So much of my life has been spent in the kitchen.

ARTHUR   I shall explain. Humanity has been increasing at an increasing rate. People have spawned people.

ALAN   Yes. They do that.

ARTHUR   And not only were men increasing their numbers, so that in three generations we should have used up the

natural resources of the world, but worse—far worse—
the poorer, more brutish sort were increasing faster than
the rest. The proportions of morons and near-morons has
been a rising curve, Mr. Armitage, because although one
can persuade intelligent people to control their numbers,
one cannot teach contraception to idiots. Idiots have more
and more outnumbered the intelligent, and under a sys-
tem of democracy, had as much political power. Lunacy!
The rain has wiped that out. Only intelligent people will
survive it, and such of the less intelligent as they choose
to carry with them.

ALAN   Why carry any?

ARTHUR   For the rough work.

ALAN   What if they refuse?

ARTHUR   They won't refuse. Does Mr. Batch refuse? Does
Captain Hunter?

ALAN   No.

ARTHUR   Do you refuse?
     (*Pause*)

ALAN   No.

ARTHUR   You know when you're well off. So do they. There
will be much for everyone to do when the waters subside,
and we begin our settlement. And with careful breeding,
inherited characteristics . . .

ALAN   Breeding?
     (*Pause*)

ARTHUR   Naturally.

ALAN   If you're so keen on breeding, why do we sleep with the men and women separated?

ARTHUR   Oh, there will be time for that, Mr. Armitage. And I do not intend, you know, to enforce a total chastity. There must be many occasions when you and Miss Banks can . . .

ALAN   We're never alone together. You know that.

ARTHUR   Surely you could make the opportunity. She spends a good deal of time alone in the hold with Mr. Batch as it is. They do their exercises together.
(*Pause*)

ALAN   What if the waters never do subside?

ARTHUR   They will. Do you imagine that natural selection intends to replace us by fish?
(*Pause*)

LECTURER   Exercises in the hold. (ALAN *and* ARTHUR *return to their seats.* TONY *and* SONYA *come into the hold area*) Begin.
(TONY *mimes his weight-lifting exercises.* SONYA *does her barre, counting to herself, "One an' two an' three an' four an' . . ."*)

SONYA   There was a boy I knew ruptured himself lifting heavy weights.

TONY   There's right and wrong ways of doing anything.

SONYA   Well, he was a bit simple. He left the show and went off with a sailor. He said he'd promised his mother he'd never marry unless it was into the navy.

TONY   Must be good for your muscles, all that, then?

SONYA   (*Counting*)   One an' two an' three an' . .

TONY   Sort of artistic, really. I done some artistic poses once for a photographer. Showing off me pectorals. I had to rub this oil all over me. Then it got on the sheets after.

SONYA   We don't do that.

TONY   That what you're doing now—do you do that in shows, like?

SONYA   No. I do modern.

TONY   (*Not understanding*)   Oh, yes?

SONYA   Do you want to see? Here, you count for me.

TONY   Count?

SONYA   Like I was doing. One an' two an' three an' . . .

TONY   (*Begins laboriously*)   One an' two an' . . .

SONYA   Only do it with a syncopated beat. A one and a two and a three and a four. And clap, eh? Like this.
(SONYA *shows him a quick, syncopated beat, clapping her hands. As he begins, she goes into a modern routine. He gets faster and faster. She can't keep up, and starts to laugh.* ALAN *leaves his seat and begins to walk slowly toward the hold area.* TONY *begins to laugh also. The routine and clapping break down, as they are both laughing.* ALAN *comes into the hold*)

ALAN   What's the joke?

SONYA   It's Tony. He can't count.

TONY   I can, then. She can't keep up.

ALAN   Sorry to interrupt. I just thought I'd see how you were getting on.

LECTURER   (*To the Audience*)   Armitage's diary is not a wholly reliable source. One has to consider that any diarist is likely to be a self-centered person who exaggerates his own importance. Armitage believed first that Arthur considered him as a possible rival, and second that Arthur deliberately encouraged an association between Miss Banks and Tony Batch so as to cripple Armitage with jealousy. If there was really a contest for leadership, it was over a trivial matter, and Armitage lost. (To *the characters*) Places for the evening discussion. Mr. Banner, Captain Hunter, you are playing "Battleships."
      (WESLEY *goes on deck as a lookout.* BANNER *and* HUNTER *begin their game at the table, watched by* MURIEL. TONY *and* SONYA *remain in the hold.* ARTHUR *goes to the cabin,* GERTRUDE *to the kitchen.* ALAN *is looking for a book*)

BANNER   A 3.

HUNTER   Miss B7.

BANNER   Hit.

ALAN   What have you done with *The Naked and the Dead?*

HUNTER   Hit what?

26

BANNER   It's on the bottom shelf—in the religious section. Aircraft carrier.

HUNTER   It can't be.

BANNER   Why not?

HUNTER   You can't have an aircraft carrier on B7. There's no room. You had a submarine on B5. Where's old Gertrude?

ALAN   Shredding twigs. She says the natives of India use them instead of toothbrushes, and have the whitest teeth in the world. She got it from the Children's Encyclopedia.

HUNTER   I brought that. It's not one of the company's books. (ALAN *has found his book*)

MURIEL   You'll not have much time for your reading. It's nearly time for study period.

BANNER   What is it tonight?

ALAN   Shakespeare.
(GERTRUDE *has come in from the kitchen.* ARTHUR *leaves the cabin and joins them, at first unobserved*)

GERTRUDE   Can I be doing it wrong? The twigs won't shred. All that happens when I clean my teeth is that I get a mouthful of bark.

ARTHUR   You need a special sort of wood, Miss Forbes-Cooper. You should have read further into the encyclopedia.

MURIEL   Arthur knows. Arthur always knows.

GERTRUDE   Arthur, how foolish of me! I am truly sorry.

ARTHUR   No, no, Miss Forbes-Cooper. We learn by doing. Where are the others?

MURIEL   Wesley's doing lookout. It's his task.

ARTHUR   (*Smiles*)   And no doubt Mr. Batch and Miss Banks are . . . practicing together?

HUNTER   Always at it.

MURIEL   Yes, they are.

ALAN   What do you mean by that?

HUNTER   Always at it. Exercises. I thought I might do it.

ALAN   Then why don't you?

HUNTER   Two's company.

MURIEL   That's right.

ALAN   I think you should be careful what you're saying.

HUNTER   Don't see *you* down there, by George.

ALAN   I do the cooking. You know that.

HUNTER   There you are, then.

ALAN   If you want to do exercises, then do them. Don't hang around hinting.

HUNTER   Who's hinting? I'm not hinting.

ALAN   They'd be glad to have you, if you want to know. I was down there myself. They asked me. I watched for a bit, and came back. Any one of us can go down at any time. Watch, join in, or anything. So you can keep your insinuations, and stuff them. Right?

ARTHUR   I agree. Captain Hunter, you will not upset Mr. Armitage. He is too busy with the cooking to make frequent trips to see what goes on in the hold, but he is glad, as we all are, that Miss Banks has found a friend. Meanwhile, please call them, Miss Forbes-Cooper. I wish to hold a conference on a minor matter.
    (GERTRUDE *goes to where the door is imagined to be, opens it, but keeps out of the wet. She calls*)

GERTRUDE   Sonya! Tony! Arthur wants you.

MURIEL   Wesley!

ARTHUR (*To* WESLEY)   Make your report, Mr. Otterdale.

WESLEY   Mine eyes have seen nothing.

ARTHUR   Then sit down, everybody, and attend. (*They compose themselves roughly as an audience, though there must be room for chairs to be moved, as will appear*) I have been considering the problem of damp. Who here has any ideas to contribute on that subject?
    (*Pause. They look at each other*)

MURIEL   Uh—Wesley's got foot rot. I haven't liked to say. And it's not healthy, never having dry underwear.

ARTHUR   The problem is solved. We shall light the stove one day a week.

SONYA   Oh, lovely!

29

ARTHUR   We shall use some of the wooden crates in the hold to start the fire. Perhaps Glub itself will burn. Then we shall stack wet driftwood against the stove to dry, when it will be burned in its turn, and dry other driftwood.

GERTRUDE   Dear Arthur! At all times so far-seeing!

ARTHUR   The thought came to me this afternoon.

HUNTER   That's old Arthur's task, by George. Thinking, that's *his* task. Does it all the time, too. No rest periods.

ALAN   Well, we can all think, I hope.

HUNTER   Not our task, though, is it?

ALAN   There's plenty of driftwood. We can have the stove going all the time once it's started. Stupid just to do it once a week.

ARTHUR   You find my arrangements stupid, Mr. Armitage?

ALAN   Well, it's not really an arrangement yet, is it? I mean, we're still discussing it.

ARTHUR   No. *You* are still discussing it.
        (Silence. GERTRUDE *moves away from* ALAN)

ALAN   Dammit, we can discuss it, Arthur. Kick it around a bit.

MURIEL   Excuse me.
        (MURIEL *moves away from* ALAN)

ALAN   Arthur, I'm not opposing you or anything. All I'm saying is that we can quite easily . . .

ARTHUR   I'm delighted to find that Mr. Armitage considers himself equally able to make decisions. It is a quality of leadership.
(BANNER *also moves away*)

BANNER (*Nervous*)   We don't disagree with Arthur here.

HUNTER   By George, no. Better not, eh?

MURIEL   Arthur knows what's good for us.
(SONYA *comes and stands beside* ALAN. TONY *does not appear to notice what is happening.* ALAN *looks at* SONYA *and then at* ARTHUR)

ALAN   Perhaps I was wrong.

ARTHUR   Are you sorry for that?

ALAN   Yes, I am sorry.

ARTHUR   It would be improvident—do you agree?—to burn *all* the wood.

ALAN   It was a very stupid suggestion. I see that now.

ARTHUR   Nevertheless, you may feel free to *make* suggestions, Mr. Armitage; I shall decide whether they be stupid or not.

ALAN   Thank you, Arthur.

ARTHUR   Ladies, and gentlemen, pray resume your former places. There is plenty of room near Mr. Armitage. (*All return to their former positions*) And now, Miss Forbes-Cooper, if you would care to proceed with the study period?

GERTRUDE   We were doing *Julius Caesar*.

ARTHUR   Caesar was a great man. He found his vocation, as I have, in middle life. (*Leaving*) Proceed, Miss Forbes-Cooper.
(GERTRUDE *comes to the front of the class.* ARTHUR *moves to the cabin*)

GERTRUDE   Would anyone like to tell me where we left off on Monday?

BANNER   We were discussing the murder of Caesar as myth.

SONYA   You said they'd all killed their father.

GERTRUDE   Quite right, my dear. Caesar was a father to the Romans, and so they killed him. Because, as Freud tells us, everyone wants to kill his father.

TONY   Ah! Well, that's wrong, isn't it?

GERTRUDE   It is not wrong, Mr. Batch. It is part of the natural order.

TONY   You take Arthur. He's like a father to us, isn't he?

BANNER   Perhaps you'd better remind us of Antony's speech, Gertrude.

GERTRUDE   Surely that isn't necessary.

BANNER   You do it so well.
(WESLEY *begins to drone*)

MURIEL   Give over now, Wesley. Gertrude's going to speak some poetry. You'll like that.

GERTRUDE   Well . . . perhaps just the beginning. I shall have to stand on something. And you can all be citizens. (BANNER *and* HUNTER *help her onto the table. Her audience stands around. She begins to declaim*) Friends, Romans, countrymen, lend me your ears. I come to bury Caesar, not . . .

LECTURER   Enough.
(*Pause.* GERTRUDE *is deflated*)

GERTRUDE   What?

LECTURER   Thank you. Enough. (BANNER *and* HUNTER *help* GERTRUDE *down again. The silence is long enough to communicate a feeling of hurt and resentment from* GERTRUDE. *They take their places in the main saloon, sitting in silence*) Mr. Armitage, the storm, please. From the beginning. (ALAN *takes a chair from the saloon, brings it out on deck. He begins to mime fishing*) As I explained in my first lecture, we do not know exactly when the rain began, because nobody noticed it. They only began to take notice when it did not stop. In its nature, it appears to have been a calm, settled downpour, with no wind. On June twenty-sixth, 1971, when the rain had continued for approximately two years, this calm was broken.

(ALAN *moves on his chair, as if the raft should be beginning to rock a little. When he notices what is happening, he is surprised. He gets up and begins to go indoors. All look up as* ALAN *goes swiftly through the main cabin and into the upstairs area*)

HUNTER   What's up? (*No reply.* ALAN *mimes knocking*) Arthur.

ARTHUR   Yes?

ALAN   Permission to speak, Arthur?

ARTHUR   Yes.

ALAN   Something's up. There's a sort of swell beginning. And there's a wind coming up.

ARTHUR   Well?

ALAN   It's been dead calm for months.

ARTHUR   Yes. (*All react as if the whole raft rocks violently*) There is some motion, certainly.
(*He gets up and comes into the main cabin*)

GERTRUDE   Arthur . . .

ARTHUR   I am going outside to see. (WESLEY *begins the same droning noise we have heard before*) Belay that, Mr. Otterdale.
(ALAN *and* ARTHUR *go on deck*)

ALAN   It's got much darker.

ARTHUR   Yes. (*Another lurching motion. All react.* ARTHUR *goes back as if to call through into the main cabin*) A distinct motion. Most distinct. Captain Hunter, come outside please.
(HUNTER *has begun to get into his oilskins*)

SONYA   What's happening?

HUNTER   Looks as if we're in for a bit of a storm. (*He goes out on deck*) I say—looks as if . . .

ARTHUR   What action do you usually take under these circumstances?

HUNTER   Get the sail down.

ARTHUR   Yes. Mr. Batch will help you.
(ALAN *goes to the door of the main cabin and calls*)

ALAN   Tony!
(TONY *gets up*)

ARTHUR   Mr. Armitage and Mr. Otterdale . . .

ALAN   . . . and Wesley, too!

ARTHUR   . . . will bring the rubber dinghy indoors. I should
not care to lose it. (*Nudged by* MURIEL, WESLEY *joins*
TONY) And after the sail?

HUNTER   I go inside, shut the door, pull the shutters down,
and go to sleep.
(*Another violent rocking.* GERTRUDE *falls over on*
MURIEL. TONY *and* WESLEY, *after it, stagger out on
deck.* MURIEL *howls*)

TONY   Muriel's cut her lip. That Gertrude fell on her.

ARTHUR   No time for that. Captain Hunter, let us begin.

HUNTER   Aye, aye, Arthur. We've got to take the sail down,
old Tone.

ARTHUR   Mr. Armitage . . .
(HUNTER *and* TONY *have begun to move, but*
HUNTER *sees something*)

HUNTER   Christ!

ARTHUR   What?

35

HUNTER (*Shouts*)   Hang on! Hang on to something! (*All dive for what is solid and nearest*) Bloody tidal wave.
(*All have violent reactions as the wave hits.* BANNER *and the women cling to the table in the cabin*)

LECTURER   Wait! (*All freeze*) It seems that there was a succession of monstrous waves. The raft would tilt as they were carried up to the crest. There the wind would hit them. Then they would slide down into a trough again—where they were at least sheltered from the wind. (*To* ASSISTANTS) Wind this time. (*To the performers*) Continue!
(ASSISTANT *leaves the stage. From now on, wind is heard when a wave hits them, diminishing in volume when they are comparatively at rest, in the trough of a wave.* WESLEY *drones when not speaking*)

ARTHUR   The dingy, Mr. Armitage.

ALAN   Come on, Wesley.

WESLEY   The Lord is mighty in anger. He sendeth the storm to chastise us.

ARTHUR   Captain Hunter . . .

HUNTER   Come on, old Tone. Get cracking, eh? (*Sees a wave approaching*) No! Wait!

ALAN   Wesley, hang on.
(*The wave hits; they recover*)

HUNTER   Right?
(WESLEY *moves forward to the center of the deck*)

WESLEY   Oh Lord, we are fit and ready for thy chastisement.

ARTHUR   Get him back. Mr. Armitage, get him back!
(TONY *and* ALAN *get him back*)

WESLEY (*Struggles against* ALAN'S *hold*)   We are thy servants, oh Lord, thy slaves and chattels. Not as we will, but
as thou wilt, oh Lord.

HUNTER   Wave!
(TONY *dives for what he has been holding on to.*
WESLEY *pulls away*)

ALAN (*Shouts above the wind*)   Hold on! Hold on, damn
you!
(WESLEY *begins to cry out, without words, in a loud
voice. He pulls against* ALAN, *who lets go. He is
blown across the deck and into the sea. He goes limp.
The wave passes*)

ARTHUR   What's happened to Mr. Otterdale?

ALAN   I was holding him.

TONY   He's gone now.

ALAN   I had to let go.

ARTHUR   Get the dinghy inside. I shall help you. Captain
Hunter, Mr. Batch, you may use a knife for the sail since
time is short. Instruct Mr. Banner to pray for succor, if he
should not already be doing so.
(TONY *and* HUNTER *get inside to cross the saloon to
reach the mast on the other side of the deck.* ARTHUR
runs quickly across to ALAN. *A wave hits. They recover*)

ALAN   He went mad, I think.

TONY (*To Banner*)   He says you got to pray.

ARTHUR   It is of no consequence. He was mad before.

BANNER   What does he wish me to say?

TONY   For succor, he says.

ARTHUR   He was expendable.

HUNTER   Come *on*, Tone.
(TONY *and* HUNTER *go out on deck to the rear.* ALAN *and* ARTHUR *have been working at the dinghy*)

ALAN   Hold on!
(*A wave hits.* TONY *and* HUNTER *grab the mast and hold on. They recover*)

HUNTER   Quick!
(TONY *and* HUNTER *mime cutting the lower rope holding the sail. Then* TONY *mounts* HUNTER'S *shoulders to cut the upper rope*)

BANNER   Oh Lord, if it be indeed thy design, as some have suggested, to punish us in this way for our misdeeds, be not too outrageous in thy wrath. Spare, oh Lord, the helpless. Bring succor to the distressed.

HUNTER   Hurry up!
(TONY *casts a scared glance at the waves, makes a slash at the rope, then drops down to the deck, clinging to the mast. A wave strikes. Then recovery. Then* ALAN *and* ARTHUR *get the dinghy on deck*)

BANNER   Consider, oh Lord, that not all have been guilty in equal measure. Consider especially the women and children. Consider . . .

ARTHUR   Inside—shutter. (TONY, ALAN, *and* HUNTER *pull across the imaginary shutter and lock it*) Why is Mr. Banner not praying?

SONYA   Book hit him.

ARTHUR   Porthole. Then find something solid and cling on.

GERTRUDE   But what of Harold?

ARTHUR   Hold him. It will do him no good to be flying about.
> (*The lights dim as the ports are closed. A wave hits; then silence*)

MURIEL   What have you done with my husband? (*Pause*) What have you done with my husband?

LECTURER (*Gently*)   No more, now. (LECTURER *moves across to the characters*) No more rain, now. Rest, now. (*Characters quietly go back to their places, watched by the* LECTURER. *When they are seated*) Sleep, now. (*Characters' heads drop.* LECTURER *advances to the audience, then speaks* (*to* ASSISTANT) Revive him. (ASSISTANT *revives* WESLEY, *and points the way offstage;* WESLEY *goes, moving like an automaton*) Nobody in this hall has committed a criminal offense, or you would not of course be here. Consequently you may not realize that what you witness is not only a history lecture, but also a necessary part of the reconditioning of some unhappy people who have committed crimes against the community. In each case the criminal's offense has a parallel in the historical person he is presenting. Thus your Arthur Henderson has been guilty of persistently individualistic behavior.

Your Alan Armitage has a history of petty crime—lack of group effort, psychosomatic asthma, public sarcasm. Both your Captain Hunter and your Sonya Banks have been guilty of private pleasure and irrational enjoyment, leading to the neglect of tasks. Your Gertrude Forbes-Cooper is a persistent liar, your Muriel Otterdale a murderess, your Tony Batch has been either late for or absent from community meetings ever since he was old enough to attend them, and your Harold Banner suffers from doubt, leading often to despair. In volunteering to present these characters, the criminals concerned are able to act out their own anticommunal tendencies, providing not only instruction for you, but therapy for themselves. (*To characters*) Wake. (*They do so; to the audience*) Now the sun shone, and the air was still. The raft lay becalmed. The sail hung from the mast like old washing. Since the raft did not move, the batteries which provided light and heat were not recharged. (*To the characters*) Days in the sun. The Beginning Time. (*They begin to take up places.* GERTRUDE *and* HAROLD *arrange a couple of chairs as backrests for sunbathing on the deck.* HUNTER *takes his spear and begins a patrol up and down one side of the deck.* ALAN *goes into the kitchen,* ARTHUR *upstairs;* MURIEL *remains at the table.* TONY *and* SONYA *go to the hold and begin their exercises*) You begin to reveal yourselves a little.

BANNER   It is true I had no vocation, but I thought I might do some good in the world.

GERTRUDE   I never married, you know. Nobody lasted long enough for me.

BANNER   I wanted to be of use.

GERTRUDE   Sir Laurence Olivier once told me I was too
intense for life. Born for the theater, not for life, he said.
But then he had to be polite, because he was turning me
down for a part.
   (ALAN *stands at the entrance to the hold and watches*
   TONY *and* SONYA, *who see him almost at once and
   stop what they are doing*)

ALAN   Here you are, then.

SONYA   Yes.

ALAN   Busy?

SONYA   Not really.

ALAN   I thought I might do it for a bit.

SONYA   You want to do weight-lifting?

ALAN   It's good for you, isn't it?
   (*Pause.* TONY *and* SONYA *exchange an uncomfortable glance*)

TONY   You don't want to do too much at first, you know.

ALAN   No?

TONY   Could do yourself a damage. Hernia or something. I
mean, it's been known.

ALAN   I'll do something simple, then.

TONY   You could try push-ups, I suppose.

ALAN   All right. I'll try push-ups.
   (*Pause.* TONY *motions him to get into position, and*

ALAN *does so. Meanwhile* MURIEL *leaves her place at the table and waits outside* ARTHUR's *door*)

BANNER You might say I drifted into the Church—an apt enough metaphor for a rowing man. I rowed for Oxford in my second year and won my rowing blue. Nobody had taken much notice of me up to then but the Moral Rearmament people were keen to recruit athletic personalities. They asked me to tea at St. Peter's Hall. There was a rugger blue and a boxing blue and two South Africans and a peer. We had strawberries and cream, and confessed our sins.

GERTRUDE But the belief? Dogma?

BANNER Oh, there's a very wide latitude of belief in the Church of England nowadays. The important thing was to do good. And really, you know, I was so busy with the Youth Club, and the Suicide Service, and Meals on Wheels, and pensioners' evenings, I had little time to think about religious questions. And when I did, I discovered that most things could be explained quite simply. All those doubts people used to have in Victorian novels. There was never any need for them now that any competent biologist can duplicate the Virgin Birth with a darning needle, and people are being raised from the dead every day. In any case, nobody wanted me to believe in God as a person, or in Christ as anything else. Nowadays, Heaven is not a place, you know, but a oneness with God. The individual soul just dissolves into the God soul. Not an easy thing to explain to my parishioners, but I didn't have to, because they never came to church.

ARTHUR What do you want, Mrs. Otterdale?

MURIEL Just to tell you.

ARTHUR What?

MURIEL I'd always do anything *you* wanted, Arthur. You've only to ask.

ARTHUR I know it. Thank you, Mrs. Otterdale.
(ALAN *has been lying in position, occasionally lifting himself a little way, but not completing a push-up*)

TONY Come on, then. (*Counting*) Seven—eight—
(ALAN *makes another attempt. Then he gets out of position and sits up*)

ALAN I can't do it.

TONY You can do *ten*.

ALAN (*Near tears*) I can't.

HUNTER (*Shouts*) Land ho!
(HUNTER *has seen something in the distance, downstage, on the* LECTURER's *side of the stage. As the others react to his cry, the* LECTURER *stops them*)

LECTURER Wait! Boarding party, remain: places, the rest. (*To the audience*) Armitage's diary reports that they had seen an ark. There was a man aboard. We know little about him—certainly not enough to create a personality. Consequently he will be presented to you by the university staff. (*To the boarding party*) You have boarded the ark. You smell the stench of it.

ARTHUR Something has died. And not recently. Good.

ALAN Good?

43

ARTHUR   Whatever has died has not been cleared away. Perhaps that is because there is nobody to clear it.

LECTURER   There is somebody. An old man appears. (ASSISTANT *moves forward*) His eyes are red in a face encrusted with filth and set in a frame of matted hair. Catch him before he falls. (*They do so*) His mouth opens, but he is parched, and cannot speak.

ARTHUR   Give him water. (ALAN *supports* ASSISTANT *gently and helps him to drink*) Who is aboard your ark, old man? (LECTURER *answers for the old man, but does not act. His voice is flat, as if reading a report*)

LECTURER   Dead. All dead.

ARTHUR   Did you have livestock? Cows? Pigs? Chickens even?

LECTURER   All dead. There was no water. And they had fouled their quarters.

ARTHUR   You had better take a look round, Mr. Armitage. (ALAN *ceases to support the* ASSISTANT)

LECTURER   I have drunk blood. Blood. I have drunk blood.

ARTHUR   See if you can find anything that may be of use. (ALAN *summons his resolution, and goes quickly through the imaginary door to the extreme side of the stage*)

LECTURER   Ham . . . Shem . . . Both dead. My wife left me, you know, before the word was fulfilled. Forty days and forty nights, I lost count. She took Japhet and went to her married sister in Scotland. More has occurred than was foretold.

ARTHUR (*Calls*)   What do you find, Mr. Armitage?

ALAN (*Returns*)   Animals all dead. Sacks of grain rotting. But there's some seed in bins.

ARTHUR   In what condition?

ALAN   I opened one. Looks all right.

ARTHUR   Can we take them?

ALAN   Too big. Sink the dinghy.

ARTHUR (*Thinks*)   Very well. I shall devise something. There are sacks on the raft. We shall transship. Meanwhile we can return.

ALAN (*Indicating the* ASSISTANT)   What about him?

ARTHUR   He is in no state to be moved.

ALAN   Do we come back for him?

ARTHUR   Unless you would prefer to remain.

ALAN   Shall I leave the water bottle?

ARTHUR   If you wish.

LECTURER   It was not the true voice I heard. When we were very thirsty, we drank the blood of the Shetland pony. I knew then it was not the true voice.

ALAN (*To* ASSISTANT) We'll be back. Just wait.
(ALAN *begins to make his return, but is cut off by the* LECTURER)

LECTURER Enough. Places. (ALAN *and* ARTHUR *begin to return to their chairs.* LECTURER *stops* ARTHUR, *who halts and half-turns*) Arthur!

ARTHUR Yes?

LECTURER What will you do with the old man?

ARTHUR Oh . . . Kill him, of course.
(ARTHUR *proceeds to his chair*)

LECTURER (*To the audience*) They transshipped the grain. It took two days. On the second night, the ark caught fire.
(LECTURER *nods to* ASSISTANT, *who gives a long scream. The cast have been sitting as if asleep on their chairs, but at the first scream* ALAN *wakes, listens, then moves forward into the main cabin, and then on deck. When he reaches the deck, he runs forward to the edge, gazing toward the lectern.* MURIEL *wakes, sees* ALAN *going, and follows him unobserved*)

ALAN The bastard! The rotten bastard!

MURIEL You shouldn't speak against Arthur like that.

ALAN Speak against him! Don't you see what he's done? Look at the ark burning. That's not an accident.

MURIEL Arthur does what he has to do.

46

ALAN And the old man?

MURIEL That's as may be.

ALAN Arthur's murdered him.

MURIEL Oh yes. My husband too.
 (*Pause*)

ALAN What?

MURIEL Wesley too. You know that.

ALAN But Wesley . . . blew away.

MURIEL No. Arthur took care of that. I know. Arthur
 takes what he wants. After all, he has to, hasn't he, if
 we're to respect him?
 (*She nods wisely and goes back in.* ALAN *follows her.*
 LECTURER *stops him*)

LECTURER Wait. (ALAN *obeys*) Will you protest?

ALAN No.

LECTURER Tell me what you are thinking.

ALAN What's the point?

LECTURER Of what?

ALAN Human life. Everything. Look. (*Turning to him*)
 You're born; you grow old; you die. You feed and sleep,
 and go to work every week, and take a holiday once a year.
 You raise children, and they grow up and leave you, and
 you're left alone. Much of your life is spent in discomfort,
 and more in boredom, and most in indifference. All you

47

have to expect is monotony and struggle while you're working, and loneliness and fear in your old age. And what's it all for? You don't really believe that making things, and packing them up, and moving them about, and selling them, and buying them, and consuming them, and making new things to replace them, add up to a reason for living. But you go on—keeping alive—because you're afraid of death. If Arthur knows what he wants, and why he wants it, what can I do?

LECTURER You do not speak of your jealousy?

ALAN No. I watch. I listen. I try to overhear. (*Pause*) I imagine.

LECTURER Why not speak to her?

ALAN We're never alone together.

LECTURER Miss Banks! (*To* ALAN) Now you are alone.
    (SONYA *comes to* ALAN)

ALAN (*To* LECTURER) I remember . . . it's very faint what I remember. Not clear. I know there was a time . . . I know we weren't together for so long.

LECTURER Three weeks.

ALAN There's a lot before that I don't know . . . I don't remember.

SONYA Three weeks.

ALAN (*To* SONYA) Just drifting. Going hungry mostly. I remember that we were happy. We sang a lot. We made love.

SONYA   Yes.

ALAN   I'd never known anything like it. Sex had been—
been *having* people—imposing myself. I'd never felt so
close. We're not close here. We're never even alone together.

SONYA   We're alone now.

ALAN   Someone might come.
(*Pause*)

SONYA   What do you want to say? (*Pause*) Do you think
I don't miss *you?* Do you think I don't want to be alone
with *you?*
(*He comes to her tentatively. They kiss, at first tentatively, then more fiercely, then as closely as they
can*)

ALAN (*With a sort of laugh*)   And they say a starvation diet
keeps your thoughts off sex!
(*He begins gently to persuade her to the ground, but
she pulls away*)

SONYA   No. Not now.

ALAN   Not?

SONYA   Let's just . . . be together for a bit. Sex—it's not
that important.

ALAN   Oh, it is.

SONYA   It's just sex. We can have sex any time.

ALAN   No, we can't. You know we can't.

SONYA No, but . . . I mean, I don't see why it has to be the first thing . . . I mean, if two people love each other . . .

ALAN They make love.

SONYA They don't have to, that's the point. If they love each other, they don't *have* to.

ALAN But, love, I want to. We both want to. I ache for it.

SONYA We never talk. Not you and me. We never get the chance. Tony's the only person I ever talk to.

ALAN Ah, yes; Tony. You are alone with him, of course. Very convenient.
(*Pause*)

SONYA We don't have to be.

ALAN You don't encourage visitors. I was humiliated, as I remember.

SONYA Not humiliated.

ALAN What would you call it?

SONYA He was trying to help. (*Pause*) Anyway, why should we spend our time talking about Tony?

ALAN He interests me. (*Pause*) What *about* Tony anyway? How about him? Is sex the first thing in *his* mind, would you say?

SONYA Of course not.

ALAN Why not? He's not queer?

SONYA   No.

ALAN   Ah, you know that, then?

SONYA   Sex doesn't come into it. I don't love Tony. We get on; that's all. He's more my kind of person than . . .

ALAN   I am?
(*Pause*)

SONYA   Yes, in a way. But I don't love him.

ALAN   I don't see why that should stop you. If sex isn't that important.

SONYA   Stop it.

ALAN   Do you think I don't wonder what you do together? Do you think I don't sit here and wonder?

SONYA   You know what we do. We do our exercises.

ALAN   You could do your exercises up here. On deck.

SONYA   We could, but we don't.

ALAN   (*Bursts out*)   "We"! "We"! You and Tony aren't "we." You and I are "we."

SONYA   Well, behave like it, then. Trust me for a start.

ALAN   Trust!

SONYA   Why should that be difficult?

ALAN   I'll tell you.

SONYA   Pray do.

ALAN   You and I—we'd never met before I found you in
that dinghy. We made love that same night. You didn't
"hold back" or anything. You didn't want just to "be" together. Nothing like that. We dived into sex. We pulled
it up over our heads and drowned in it. And you were a
bloody sight better than I was. More experienced. But I
suppose that's because it was "just sex," eh? Not *that* important.

SONYA   And?

ALAN   If me, why not Tony? If so *soon* with me, so quick
with me?
   (*Pause*)

SONYA   I think I'll go in now. I've gone off you. Funny! I
came out to tell you something. It's rather important, actually. I've been saving it to tell you. Nobody else knows.

ALAN   Not even Tony?

SONYA   I'm pregnant.
   (*Pause*)

ALAN   What?

SONYA   I thought you'd be pleased. I was *that* stupid.

ALAN   But I am. I am, love. I am. I am pleased.

SONYA   Are you? Well, that won't last, will it? After all, you
don't know whose it is.
   (*She turns her back on him and goes inside. He
   watches her*)

LECTURER *(To the cast)*   Go on to the morning of August third.

(The characters dispose themselves on deck. ARTHUR *comes briskly out on deck, followed by* MURIEL, *who brings a chair and the logbook with her.* ARTHUR *claps his hands)*

ARTHUR   I have decided to call the first meeting of the new society. *(To* MURIEL*)* Thank you, Mrs. Otterdale. Set it there, if you please. *(She sets the chair for him)* Have you the logbook? Sit down. *(She does so; he continues)* This will be our minute book. I shall now enter the minutes of our first meeting. By this means, we shall have a record of our society from the beginning. *(He sits, produces a pencil, and begins to write)* Minutes of the first meeting of the New Society. August third, 1971. Present . . .
(He continues to write)

ALAN   But we've no livestock. No scientific skills. How . . . ?

ARTHUR *(While writing)*   There will be a time for questions later, Mr. Armitage. Meanwhile I have not yet declared the meeting open. *(Finishes)* The meeting is open. I propose that the society be called the New Society. All in favor?
(All raise their hands)

BANNER   Aye.

ARTHUR   Good. *(Writing)* Officers. We should not, in my view, burden ourselves with too many at first. One officer, to be called the president, and to combine the duties of president, secretary, and treasurer, should suffice. That is my proposal. All in favor?
(All raise their hands)

53

HUNTER   Aye, aye.

BANNER   (*Hesitantly*) I should like to propose Arthur for president.

ARTHUR   Who seconds?

ALAN   I do.

ARTHUR   All in favor? (*All raise their hands.* ARTHUR *writes*) *Nemine contra dicente.* Next . . .

ALAN   Do you think there should be any provision for a deputy president?

ARTHUR   Why?

ALAN   In case anything were to happen to you, Mr. President.

ARTHUR   Nothing will. Now . . . Rules. As your president, I shall promulgate rules from time to time. Rule one: Doubt can disable us. Any part of the body politic which doubts its survival must be cut out.

ALAN   Ah!

ARTHUR   You spoke?

ALAN   Just breathing.

ARTHUR   Breathe more quietly. Any questions?

ALAN   None.

ARTHUR   Rule Two: While we remain becalmed, we shall cut down on the use of power. No lights will be used. We

Act One—John Colenback as ALAN ARMITAGE and Gretchen Gorbett as SONYA BANKS.

shall rise with the sun and retire with it. Furthermore, there will be no cooking. We have been becalmed for two months. We must conserve power. Heat will be used only to distill water.

HUNTER   No stew. Just eat Glub?

ARTHUR   Impractical! We shall do better with fish. Only we must make shift with it *au bleu*.

BANNER   Blue?

ARTHUR   Raw.

HUNTER   Eat raw fish?

ARTHUR   It is not unknown.

BANNER   I suppose . . . it might be almost Japanese.

ARTHUR   Exactly. A great delicacy—properly regarded. And seaweed also. (*Hubbub among the characters*) Settle down . . . Lastly . . .

LECTURER   Right. (*To the audience*) The new rule was put into effect that night. (*To the cast*) Fish supper. (*All take their places for supper*)

ARTHUR   Sit down, Mr. Banner, please ask a blessing.

BANNER (*Doleful*)   For what we are about to receive may the Lord make us truly thankful.

ARTHUR   Amen. (*A pause. All look at* ARTHUR. *He tastes the fish*) It is unpleasant on the whole. (HUNTER *and* BANNER *taste*)

55

BANNER The Japanese . . .

HUNTER There's always been something fishy about the Japanese.
(ALAN, TONY, MURIEL, *and* GERTRUDE *taste and swallow.* SONYA *does not. All look at her*)

ARTHUR Come now, Miss Banks.
(SONYA *lifts a spoonful toward her mouth, pauses, then puts it back on the plate*)

SONYA I don't fancy it.

ARTHUR It will do you good.

SONYA Not if I bring it all up again, it won't.

ARTHUR You must keep it down.

SONYA I can't. I don't want any. Anybody can have mine.

ARTHUR (*Looking round*) There is no need for us all to stop eating, just because Miss Banks is having a little difficulty with her fish. (*All begin eating again*) Now, Miss Banks, we must eat our fish, let us try again.

MURIEL Must eat our nice fish.

GERTRUDE Yes, indeed. Delicious.

ALAN I don't see why she should be forced to eat. It's her own funeral.

ARTHUR But while she is in my charge, I do not intend her funeral to take place.

ALAN Couldn't she have . . .

56

ARTHUR   There will be no exceptions.

ALAN   Sorry.

ARTHUR   Sorrow by itself means nothing, unless it is accompanied by the intention of amendment. Do not interfere again. (*To* SONYA, *blazing out*) *Eat your fish!*
(*Shocked silence. Then all but* SONYA *and* TONY— *who is eating normally—begin to eat at double time.* SONYA *lifts a spoonful toward her mouth again*)

TONY (*Gently*)   Come on, then, old Sonn, eh?
(*Her spoon follows his in time. She takes a mouthful, chews, and swallows*)

ARTHUR   Excellent, excellent! Now, all together. With me. Begin.
(*All begin eating in time with* ARTHUR)

LECTURER   Enough! (*All stop*) The water ration was reduced. Raw fish gave everyone diarrhea. They grew weaker. The sun brought out self-doubts like bubbles on a tarred roof, which grew, and burst, and grew again. (*To the cast*) Days in the Sun. The Middle Time.
(HUNTER, GERTRUDE, *and* BANNER *have appeared with chairs which they arrange for sunbathing.* ALAN *stays where he is.* TONY *and* SONYA *go into the hold area for their exercises.* MURIEL *watches* ALAN *and the sunbathers from a little distance*)

BANNER   I found I couldn't communicate, do you see? There were problems of language. Among the criminal classes, the word "bird" for instance is used to mean "lady friend" and also a stretch in prison. So that the expression "to do one's bird" was only confusing.

GERTRUDE   I played Antigone when I was only twenty-four. Bernard Shaw sent me orchids and Doctor Ernest Jones took me out to lunch.
    (SONYA *laughs*)

MURIEL   They're down there.

ALAN   I know.

MURIEL   They're always down there.

GERTRUDE   Six years ago, I went back to the same theater. My agent said it would be a comeback for me, I was the parson's wife in a comedy about sailors—not a large part, by no means large. I'd written "Gertrude Forbes-Cooper, Actress" in greasepaint on the wall of my dressing room. It was still there, so I crossed out the "Actress."

HUNTER   I used to wonder what was going to happen to all the chaps like me. I mean, if you're not bright, where are you going to go? I used to look at middle-aged chaps in the subway, on buses; I used to think, "*You're* like me. *You're* not bright. You'll go under. Bound to."

GERTRUDE   The theater! That feeling one had sometimes in the theater, that wonderful thrill, almost of reverence, a prickling of the back hairs.

BANNER   Yes.

GERTRUDE   I discovered it could be self-induced.

BANNER   But surely one learns from the theater, does one not?

ALAN   Learns what?

58

BANNER   About the nature of life?

ALAN   You'd learn more about life from one week as a probation officer than ten years of heavy theater-going.

MURIEL   We are in a bad temper, aren't we?

GERTRUDE   Arthur sees these things so differently. It is a matter of proportion, he says.

BANNER   Of control.

GERTRUDE   Of seeing things in proportion.

HUNTER   "*Down* you go," I'd think. "They'll automate the lot of you. Rabbits!"

ALAN   Oh, Arthur! Arthur!

BANNER   It is a matter of control.

ALAN   How can Arthur or anyone else . . .

GERTRUDE   Arthur will look after things. It is only a matter of obeying.

MURIEL   Arthur knows what's right.

BANNER   Exactly. Exactly.

ALAN   How? How does he know?

HUNTER   Well, I mean there's a place for everybody with Arthur.

MURIEL   Arthur knows what's best for all of us.

ALAN A murderer! (*Silence.* ARTHUR *gets up from his chair*) Arthur's our leader, and we depend on him, but he's not a god. He's not above doing foolish and wicked things, you know that. It wouldn't have hurt us to have taken that old man from the ark, but Arthur murdered him.
(*Pause*)

BANNER How hot it is!

GERTRUDE I remember that as a very *little* girl, I could lie all day in the sun. Mother always said I was storing up energy for the winter.

ALAN (*Near tears*) You don't want to hear. You're afraid of being upset.

GERTRUDE But we're not afraid of anything, while Arthur is here to look after us.
(MURIEL *leaves the deck area and goes to the cabin. She knocks*)

ARTHUR Come in, Mrs. Otterdale. (*She does so*) Make your report.

MURIEL They're carrying on.

ARTHUR Who?

MURIEL That Sonya and Tony. *He* knows. He can't keep his mind off it when they're together.

ARTHUR No self-discipline. He deserves what he gets.

MURIEL What are you going to do about it, Arthur?

ARTHUR   Permit it.

MURIEL   But they're carrying on.

ARTHUR   It is of no consequence. If Miss Banks is carrying on now, she can have less objections to being shared later.

MURIEL   Shall I be shared, Arthur?

ARTHUR   Of course.

MURIEL   (*A horrid little giggle*)   It'll make a change. Will Gertrude be . . .

ARTHUR   All the women will be shared. In the New Society we shall all love one another. Equally.

MURIEL   But you most, Arthur.

ARTHUR   First, Mrs. Otterdale, not most. There is a distinction. What else do you have to tell me?

MURIEL   He's been talking against you.

ARTHUR   Mr. Armitage? In what way?

MURIEL   He said you were a murderer. He said you did foolish and wicked things. He said you weren't a god.

ARTHUR   Foolish?

MURIEL   That's what he said.

ARTHUR   What can he have meant by foolish?

MURIEL Foolish and wicked, he said. He told Harold and Gertrude.

ARTHUR What did they reply?

MURIEL They said it was very hot.

ARTHUR Foolish? I should be angry if I did not consider the source.

MURIEL What'll you do to him, then?

ARTHUR Nothing. Mr. Armitage is without convictions and without a backbone. He does no harm. Meanwhile we can use a cook. And you might look more closely at Miss Banks, my dear. She is concealing something.

MURIEL Yes, Arthur. (*Pause*) There's nothing else, Arthur.

ARTHUR Nothing?

MURIEL Unless . . . *you* wanted anything . . .
    (ARTHUR *takes her by the shoulders*)

ARTHUR You must not be coy, my dear. It is not becoming in a widow of your years. (*He embraces her, in the manner of one who takes but does not share*) But you must be very quiet. (*He kisses her again, then breaks away*) Not a god, he said?

MURIEL I'll lie down, shall I?

LECTURER Enough. The evening meal now. (*As they take their places, he addresses the audience*) The change from an autocratic to a theocratic society began that evening at supper.

ARTHUR   I have been thinking about myth.

GERTRUDE   Myth . . . Yes . . .

ARTHUR   We are all of us in a mythological situation, are we not?

BANNER   Er . . .

ARTHUR   We are the people who came out of the sea. A new race will spring, as it were, from our loins.

TONY   Loins?

ALAN   Sex.

TONY   Oh.

MURIEL   Shhh!

ARTHUR   Consider our descendants. For their own self-respect, they must remember us as greater than we are. *We* may know that we are quite ordinary beings . . .

GERTRUDE   No, no, Arthur.

MURIEL   Not you, Arthur.

HUNTER   Not Arthur, by George.

ARTHUR   Thank you. (*A little smile*) However.

BANNER   Do please continue, Arthur.

ARTHUR   We may know that we are human. But if we
are to found a race, they may wish to think of us as gods.
And it may be good for them to think so. It will encourage morality and right behavior.

TONY   Gods? Us?

ARTHUR   And goddesses, of course.
(He gives a permissive nod to the women)

SONYA   Thank you.

ARTHUR   Cooks in the future may light a candle to Mr.
Armitage—and as for me . . .

GERTRUDE   Yes, Arthur.

ARTHUR   Our descendants may think of *me* as the leader
of all. The source of all power and benefits. They may
do that.

GERTRUDE   Oh, they will. They will.

ARTHUR   What make a god? Any thinking person will tell
you that men make their own. They do so by worship.
Whatever you worship is god, whether it be a tree, or the
sun, or two sticks, or a bull, or a ring of stones. Simple
men worship the things themselves. Complicated men
worship the ideas the things express. But ultimately it
makes little difference. The behavior—the ritual—is
what matters. Interpretations may change, but the ritual
endures. Is that not so, Mr. Banner?

BANNER   Very largely, Arthur.

ARTHUR   Very largely?

BANNER Entirely.

ARTHUR Good. (*Looks around the table*) You had better begin by worshiping me. Some of you may feel that I am unworthy. You must conquer that feeling. It will, in any case, die with you, while what is recorded of your behavior will live on as revealed religion. Any questions? (*Pause*)

ALAN No questions.

ARTHUR Then we shall begin our meal. Mr. Banner, please ask a blessing.
(BANNER *looks timidly at* ARTHUR, *who gives him an encouraging nod*)

BANNER For what we are about to receive, may Arthur make us truly thankful.

ARTHUR Quite right. And so I do.
(*They begin to mime eating.* TONY *is obviously puzzled by the whole proceedings, but joins in with the rest. They stop as the* LECTURER *speaks*)

LECTURER They required a wind, so that the raft would be propelled through the sea, and its batteries be recharged, and they would have heat again to distill water, and cook their food. Arthur told them that they must behave in a manner appropriate to the myth in which they were participating. They must attempt to raise a wind by magic. They did so. (GERTRUDE *goes to the deck area, where she beats an imaginary rag against the imaginary mast, continuing to do this through the action until indicated*) They beat a wet rag against metal, but there was no wind. (MURIEL *goes out on deck and swooshes an imaginary bowl around*) They filled a bowl with sea water and rocked it about to make waves in sympathetic magic, but the waves lacked sympathy, and there was no wind. (HUNTER *goes to the front of the deck area and begins to whistle mournfully*) They whistled. (ALAN, TONY, BANNER, *and* ARTHUR *join* HUNTER *in whistling*) The men all whistled for a wind. (SONYA *joins them, and* GERTRUDE *and* MURIEL *begin to whistle where they are*) And the women whistled for a wind, but the wind did not reply.

(ARTHUR *watches for a moment, then*)

ARTHUR Stop. What next?

ALAN They used to nail a gold piece to the mast.

ARTHUR They?

ALAN People. Primitive people.

ARTHUR Mr. Batch, pray instruct Miss Forbes-Cooper to cease whistling and join us. Perhaps someone has a gold piece with them? (*Pause. Nobody has*) Or any gold object?

MURIEL I've got two pounds.

ARTHUR Yes.

MURIEL Nine and seven.

ARTHUR Get it. Captain Hunter, pray fetch a hammer, proceed to the mast and prepare to nail.

HUNTER Aye, aye, Arthur.

(HUNTER *goes off to the hold area for a hammer*

and a nail. MURIEL *feels furtively inside her clothing and gets out imaginary money)*

ALAN   They threw money into the sea too. A sort of offering.

ARTHUR (*Taking the money from* MURIEL)   Then we shall divide the money. Mr. Batch, you will assist Captain Hunter to nail this pound note as high up the mast as possible. We shall throw the remaining one pound nine and seven simultaneously into the sea. Is there anything else, Mr. Armitage, while you think of it?

ALAN   Not unless you have anybody in mind for Iphigenia.

ARTHUR   Iphigenia? I don't understand you.

ALAN   Oh, it wasn't a serious suggestion. I'm afraid you'd need a real child if you were going to sacrifice to . . .
(*He stops himself, horrified.* SONYA's *hands have gone to her belly. They gaze at each other.* ARTHUR *notices.* BANNER *does not, and goes on)*

BANNER   The reference, Arthur, is to King Agamemnon, who sacrificed his own daughter when the Greeks lay becalmed at Aulis.

ALAN   I said it wasn't a serious suggestion.
(HUNTER *goes to the mast with an imaginary hammer and nail.* TONY *gets up on his shoulders and prepares to nail the pound note while* ARTHUR *draws the rest of the crew into a half-circle to watch him offer the money)*

ARTHUR   Ready, Mr. Batch?

TONY   O.K.

ARTHUR   Right. I suppose notes will be acceptable.
(*He throws the money.* TONY *hammers. The rest watch*)

GERTRUDE   How pretty the silver looks turning over and over—oh!

SONYA   What?

GERTRUDE   A fish has eaten the pound note.

ARTHUR   A fish has eaten the pound note. The gift has been accepted. But I imagine that we must wait a while.
(TONY *and* HUNTER *join the others*)

TONY   Hey, Arthur!

ARTHUR   Yes?

TONY   I saw something. Looked like fog or something.

ARTHUR   Fog? Impossible.

TONY   Or smoke or something. A sort of wall, all thick and cloudy. It's over there. Look.

ALAN   (*With sarcastic dislike for* TONY)   A forest fire, perhaps?

TONY   What's so funny? It could be something burning. I mean, *we* burned . . .
(*There is a hiss of indrawn breath from* BANNER, GERTRUDE, *and* MURIEL)

ARTHUR   What? What did "we" burn?

TONY   I'm not trying to make nothing of it.

ARTHUR   Then avoid the impression that you are. It does appear to be fog. And moving, as I suppose, toward us, since *we* do not move.

SONYA   Yes. You can see it now. From down here.
(*They move toward the edge of the raft, as if the fog were approaching them from the audience*)

HUNTER   Never seen fog like that before. Nothing like it in the Children's Encyclopedia.

BANNER   Out of . . . a clear sky.

HUNTER   I dare say there's an explanation if we looked it up.

BANNER   Drift . . . sea drift . . .

HUNTER   You'd look in the index. Under *F*, I dare say.

BANNER   The edge of the world was held by the ancients to be a place of fogs.
(GERTRUDE *and* MURIEL *are frightened. They move closer to* ARTHUR)

ARTHUR   The world is round. It has no edge.

BANNER   No . . . no, of course not.

SONYA   I saw a picture about Niagara Falls once. They were all steamy. Robert Ryan was in it.

ALAN   It's much closer now.

HUNTER   Be in it soon, eh?

MURIEL Arthur!

GERTRUDE Arthur, make her be quiet.

MURIEL I wish we'd never come. I wish we'd stayed at home. We don't know how thick it is or anything.

LECTURER (*To* ASSISTANT) Noise, please.
(ASSISTANT *goes offstage*)

ALAN (*Angry*) There's nothing to be frightened of. We've all flown through cloud before.

TONY What's a cloud doing down here, then?
(*A noise begins. It is a high noise on one note. It gets louder as the scene progresses, cutting out when indicated. As it begins, they listen*)

LECTURER (*To the cast*) With the noise, the water becomes suddenly choppy.
(*All stagger*)

ARTHUR This is ridiculous. There is no wind to inspire rough water.

HUNTER Hey! The water's changing color.
(*They shift the focus of their attention downward*)

SONYA It's all brown.

GERTRUDE (*A wail*) The water's poisoned. Arthur!

MURIEL It's the drowned people, poisoning the water.

ARTHUR Nonsense. It is only weed. A common phenomenon at sea. Brown weed.

ALAN   We've never seen weed before. Not like this. Covering the sea.

ARTHUR   You see it now.
(*Pause*)

SONYA   I wish I knew what that noise was.

LECTURER (*To the cast*)   A moment. (*They are still; he speaks to the audience*) They had, of course, come to what is indeed a common enough phenomenon at sea—the meeting of two currents, one warm, one cold. All this time they had thought themselves motionless, they had been drifting with one current. Now they had come to the junction, and found mist there, and a great deal of weed, and a high concentration of marine life, most of it in violent activity. (*To the cast*) Continue.

ARTHUR   I have worked things out. We are in a current. We have been drifting, and without a point of reference, could not know it.
(BANNER *sneezes*)

ALAN   Bless you.

BANNER   Thank you.

ARTHUR   Surely we were more warmly clad when we came aboard?

MURIEL   Will I get your oilskins, Arthur?

ARTHUR   No. Blankets. Blankets for all. Miss Forbes-Cooper, assist her.
(*They go to the indoors area, where* ASSISTANTS *give them blankets*)

HUNTER   Hallo!

ARTHUR   What was that?
>
> (HUNTER *goes to see, and as he does so, another lurch makes them all stagger. He picks an imaginary fish up*)

HUNTER   It's a fish. Jumped right out of the water and onto the deck. Silly little bastard must have lost his way in the fog.
>
> (GERTRUDE *and* MURIEL *reappear with blankets*)

ARTHUR   One to each, please.

HUNTER   What shall I do with the fish?

ALAN   Eat it!

HUNTER   Better to throw it back. It's undersized anyway.
>
> (*All are given blankets and wear them around their shoulders*)

ARTHUR   Has everyone been issued with blankets?

SONYA   We do look like a lot of Red Indians, I must say.

BANNER   It's getting . . . thicker.

MURIEL   Arthur, will it finish soon?

ARTHUR   Stay close to me, Mrs. Otterdale, if you are frightened.

GERTRUDE   I'm frightened too.

ARTHUR   Very well. You may come close also.

SONYA   That noise is louder too.

BANNER   I don't understand the noise. I confess I do not.
(*Another lurch, though they have been a little unsteady ever since they noticed the choppiness of the water*)

ALAN   I'm not used to this. I don't feel very well.

ARTHUR   Stay close to the side, then, and do not soil the deck.

SONYA   I'm so cold.
(ALAN *has an idea. He dips his hand over the side*)

ALAN   The water's cold. It's been warm all this time.

GERTRUDE (*A wail*)   I'm frightened.

MURIEL (*Joining in*)   Frightened!
(*They take* ARTHUR's *hands. He tries to break their hold*)

ARTHUR   Mrs. Otterdale! Miss Forbes-Cooper! Let go of my hands.

GERTRUDE   We're frightened.

MURIEL   Frightened.

ARTHUR   I must retain my freedom of action. Go inside, ladies.

MURIEL (*Sobs*)   I can't. If I can't see, I don't know what I shan't imagine.

GERTRUDE   Can't go in. Don't make us go in.
(LECTURER *now moves to them and speaks to them sharply and urgently*)

LECTURER   Fish! Fish everywhere. Jumping and leaping. Hunting and hunted. Eating and being eaten. The air and the water, thick with fish and mist, all alive, all everywhere—screaming, screaming all around. That's what you hear. You hear the fish scream.

MURIEL   I want to go home. I want to go home. (GERTRUDE *claps her hands on her breast as though a fish has jumped at her. All the following dialogue overlaps*)

GERTRUDE (*Screams*)   What is it? Oh, what is it?

MURIEL   Arthur! Save me! Arthur!
(GERTRUDE *tries to clasp* ARTHUR, *who tries to avoid her.* MURIEL, *jealous as well as frightened, tries to pull* GERTRUDE *off and clasp* ARTHUR *for herself.* HUNTER *and* BANNER *are trying to calm them down.* SONYA *moves away, her hands over her belly to protect it. Both* ALAN *and* TONY *come to her, but each stops on meeting the other. The noise continues, louder. It is a mess*)

HUNTER   It's only a fish. It's harmless.

MURIEL   Leave Arthur alone. You leave him alone.

ARTHUR   Miss Forbes-Cooper! Mrs. Otterdale!

GERTRUDE   Save me! Save me! You promised.

MURIEL   You keep off him. He's mine.

HUNTER   Harold, tell her it's only a fish.

GERTRUDE   Arthur!

ARTHUR   Unhand me.

HUNTER (*Tossing the fish away*) It's harmless. It couldn't hurt you.

ARTHUR Mr. Banner! Captain Hunter! Get rid of these women.

BANNER Come on now, Gertrude.

GERTRUDE Won't go. Don't make me go.

HUNTER and BANNER Come on.
     (*Pulling*)

GERTRUDE and MURIEL No! No! No! No!
     (*Resisting*)

MURIEL (*To* ARTHUR) You're god! You told us. Make it stop.

GERTRUDE God. You're god.

MURIEL God! God! Make it stop.

GERTRUDE God make it stop.
     (*A pause while the men wait for* ARTHUR *to respond.
     All talk has to be loud above the noise, but* ALAN *now
     speaks savagely*)

ALAN Go on, Arthur. Make it stop, if you're god.
     (*Pause*)

ARTHUR Let go your hands, women. Take your hands from my robe. (*The women let go. All watch* ARTHUR. *He goes to the edge of the deck area, spreads his blanket like wings from his shoulders, and addresses the audience*

75

area) Waters! By virtue of the authority vested in me as god, I command you to stop. (*A small pause. Then the noise cuts out*) I will have no more nonsense, waters. I command it. (*Pause*) Now, go forth and feel the waters, Mr. Armitage.

ALAN They're warm again.

BANNER God be praised. (ARTHUR *turns and looks at him*) God Arthur be praised, that is.

ARTHUR We shall go in now. There is nothing more to do here.
> (*Wearing his blanket like a robe, he walks upstage. The others fall in behind him, making a procession. The procession goes offstage completely.* LECTURER *steps forward*)

LECTURER Please break for fifteen minutes and reassemble here.

Curtain

Act Two

All the characters but ARTHUR *are on their chairs; he remains offstage.* ASSISTANTS *have removed unneeded and set needed props.* LECTURER *arrives. The house lights go down.*

LECTURER (*To the audience*) The miracle by which Arthur proved his godhead was not really a miracle. The raft had passed out of the junction area of the two currents: that is all. But to the people of the raft—and certainly to Arthur himself—it did seem miraculous. Meanwhile the sun shone. The days passed. Miss Banks' condition became obvious, and was accepted. (*An* ASSISTANT *comes to* SONYA, *and motions her to stand. He fastens to her stomach a kind of small bolster, tying it with tapes at the back. She runs her hand wonderingly over it, as if feeling the baby within her belly*) There were no more exercises, though she continued to spend time with Mr. Batch.
(SONYA *begins to sing "Flow Gently Sweet Afton" like a lullaby to herself*)

SONYA (*Singing*) Flow gently, sweet Afton, among thy green braes . . .

TONY What's that, then?

SONYA "Flow Gently Sweet Afton." Don't you know it? Come out in the sun. I'll teach you.
(SONYA *and* TONY *find a place together on the deck area, using their chairs as backrests*)

79

LECTURER (*To the audience*) The god Arthur remained incommunicado. He was growing a beard, as became his godhead. As the only clergyman, Mr. Banner became priest to the god. He prepared the god's food and was the only one allowed to see the god. (BANNER *rises and mimes a business in the kitchen area*) Mr. Armitage continued to cook for the others. (ALAN *goes to the entrance of the kitchen area and watches* BANNER *disdainfully*) Drifting gently in the warm water, remote from any society but their own, with a god now to look after them, each in his own way moved back into childhood: it was so easy. (*Gently, to* MURIEL) Play, Muriel. Go out and play now.
    (*Solemnly* MURIEL *goes out on deck and begins to mime playing a bouncing-ball game against the imaginary wall of the cabin*)

MURIEL (*Sings*)
    Bouncy, bouncy, ball-ie!
    Break a leg of doll-ie.

LECTURER Gertrude.

MURIEL (*Sings*)
    One an' two an' three an' four an' five an' six . . .
    (GERTRUDE *gets up during* MURIEL's *chant, and begins to rummage in a corner of the saloon area*)

GERTRUDE Harold.

BANNER Yes?

GERTRUDE Do you want a game?

BANNER Cards or checkers?

GERTRUDE Cards, of course, Silly-Billy.

80

BANNER   No.

GERTRUDE   Checkers, then.

BANNER   I can't. I've got to get the god his lunch.

ALAN   I'll play.

GERTRUDE   No. I want to play with Harold.
(BANNER *has carried an imaginary plate in from the
kitchen area, and sets it on the table*)

ALAN   Suit yourself.

BANNER (*To* GERTRUDE)   Help me on with my surplice.
(ALAN *goes on outside.* BANNER *gets his surplice on,
helped by* GERTRUDE, *and carries the imaginary plate
to the cabin area*)

MURIEL   I did thirty-one.

ALAN   Good.

MURIEL   You don't care, do you?

ALAN   No.

MURIEL   Bet you can't do thirty-one. Bet you can't do any.

ALAN (*Looking round*)   Where's Hunter?

MURIEL   In the toilet. He's always there; it's not fair. You
can't get in. He doesn't do anything. He just sits there,
sucking his thumb.
(BANNER *mimes knocking*)

BANNER   The servant of the god, with the god's lunch.

LECTURER   Enter and wait. You see the god before you.
(BANNER *enters the upstairs area and waits*)

SONYA (*Sings*)
Flow gently, sweet Afton,
Among thy green braes.

TONY   What's braes, then?

SONYA   I don't know. It's just in the song.
(*Sings*)
Flow gently,
I'll sing thee a song in thy praise.
(MURIEL *has been watching and has come to stand over them. Now she begins to sing in competition*)

MURIEL (*Sings*)
Root them up. Put them behind.
Four little foxes that will spoil the vine.

SONYA   Shut up. I'm trying to teach Tony a song.

MURIEL   Who's stopping you?

SONYA   He can't concentrate on one song if you're singing another.

MURIEL   Sucks! Boo! Boodleie-hoo! I've got a better song than you. (*Sings*)
Envy! Jealousy! Malice! Pride!
All if allowed will in your heart abide.

TONY (*Speaks*)   Flow gently. I'll sing thee a song in thy praise.

MURIEL (*Sings*)
> Envy! Jealousy! Malice! Pride!
> All if allowed will in your heart abide.
> (ALAN *shrugs and goes back into the saloon area*)

ALAN   What's the god having for lunch?

GERTRUDE   Well, Harold *calls* it bouillabaisse. What are we having?

ALAN   Flying fish.

SONYA (*Sings*)
> Flow gently, sweet Afton, among thy green braes
> Flow gently, I'll sing thee a song in thy praise.

TONY (*Speaks*)   Song in thy praise.

MURIEL (*Sings*)
> All if allowed will in your heart abide.

ALAN   We get better food than the god does because I'm a better cook than Harold is.

GERTRUDE (*Shocked*)   Harold isn't a cook at all. He's the priest of the god. You are awful, saying that. Harold doesn't cook. He prepares the god's repast. *You* cook.
> (LECTURER *signals* ASSISTANT, *who goes into the cabin area and whispers to* BANNER)

SONYA (*Sings*)
> My Mary's asleep by the murmuring stream.

TONY (*Speaks*)   —ring stream.

83

SONYA (*Sings*)
Flow gently, sweet Afton. Disturb not her dream.
(BANNER *comes out of the cabin area to the saloon*)

BANNER   The god wants some glue.

ALAN   What's he want glue for?

BANNER   He didn't say.

GERTRUDE   It's better not to question the god's desires.
Whatever the god wants is good.

BANNER   He may have a use for glue. On the other hand,
he may just want it.

ALAN   There's some in the hold. I'll get it.

BANNER   No. I'll go. Otherwise it would only have to be
purified.

GERTRUDE   Now we'll miss our game.

BANNER (*Going*)   The service of the god comes before
games.
(BANNER *mimes the business of going down into the
hold and searching about*)

ALAN   I said I'd play. Let me. Why can't I play?

GERTRUDE   We'll keep a separate score, then. One for you
and one for Harold. There's no point in playing unless
you can see who's won.
(*They carry their imaginary box of checkers out onto
the deck, and set up the board*)

SONYA   Now go all through by yourself.

84

TONY (*Sings*)
Flow gently, sweet Afton, among thy green . . .

SONYA (*Prompts*)   Braes.

TONY (*Sings*)
Flow gently, I'll . . . I'll sing thee . . .

SONYA (*Prompts, singing*)
A song in thy praise.

ALAN   Can't you shut up singing that? It puts me off.

MURIEL (*With relish*)   Envy! Jealousy! Malice! Pride!

TONY (*Sings*)
My Mary's asleep by the murmuring stream.

MURIEL (*Sings*)
All if allowed will in your heart abide.

GERTRUDE   You've got to take me. And now . . . (*Moving a piece*) I . . . take . . . you. You're not much good, are you?

ALAN   I can't concentrate with Tony bawling his head off. (BANNER *has come out of the hold. He goes into the saloon area, and then to cabin, and knocks*)

BANNER   The servant of the god with glue. (*He enters. Pause.* ASSISTANT *whispers*)

GERTRUDE   Shouldn't have asked to play, then.

ALAN   Oh, for Christ's sake, why does everybody keep getting at me all the time?

GERTRUDE   Who's getting at you? *I'm* not getting at you.

MURIEL   She's not getting at you.

ALAN (*Mimicking*)   "Shouldn't have asked to play, then."
It's no pleasure playing with you.

GERTRUDE   Alan, don't struggle. You're not happy within
yourself.
    (BANNER *receives the message, comes into the saloon,
    then goes out on deck*)

ALAN (*Angry*)   Yes, I am. I'm quite happy.

GERTRUDE   If you were happy in yourself, you'd see that
the god Arthur is good and necessary, as we do.

BANNER   Just make an act of faith, dear boy. Everything
follows from that.

GERTRUDE   You'll be a different man.

ALAN   I don't want to be a different man.

BANNER   Don't you? Are you enjoying life as you are?

ALAN   What's he want with glue?

BANNER   We are to make a mask.

MURIEL   Can I help? I can help, can't I? I'll help.

BANNER   We can all help, as an act of devotion. We soak
paper in glue, and it turns into papier-mâché. Then we
mould it.

ALAN   What does he want a mask for?

86

Act Two—Alan MacNaughtan as HAROLD BANNER, Nancy Marchand as GERTRUDE FORBES-COOPER, Maureen Pryor as MURIEL OTTERDALE, Paul Sparer as the LECTURER, Bill Burns as TONY BATCH, Alec McCowen as ARTHUR HENDERSON, and Anthony Oliver as CAPTAIN HUNTER.

MURIEL Questions! Always asking questions!

BANNER He says his face is too terrible for us to see.

ALAN What's happened to his face?

GERTRUDE It is the face of a god. Of course it's terrible. It must be.

ALAN Harold sees it.

BANNER Not lately. He hides it under the sheet. He says we're to make eyeholes and a mouth. This is going to be a smiling mask, but later on we may have to make a frowning one.

GERTRUDE Oh, Harold, I hope he will never appear to us in a frowning mask.

MURIEL (*To* ALAN) Not to us, but he may to some.

LECTURER (*To* ASSISTANTS) Bring on the god. (ASSISTANTS *go offstage. Characters face upstage in silence, and wait;* LECTURER *speaks to the audience*) They soaked pages of the *Condensed Guide to the World's Great Books* in a pot with glue, and made a mask. The god kept to his own small room and was not seen outside. (ASSISTANTS *bring* ARTHUR *on. He is masked, and his beard protrudes outside the mask. He walks like a sleepwalker, guided by the* ASSISTANTS, *who stand him on his stool.* LECTURER *speaks to the audience*) It was hot in the god's holy place, and close, and being a god, he could not wash or visit the lavatory, except privately, so the atmosphere became unpleasant. (BANNER *marshals all the others except* HUNTER *in a group outside the upstairs area*) Mr. Banner brought the worshipers into the god's presence.

BANNER   Now, remember. When you get into the presence, kneel, and bow your heads. (*He looks around for* HUNTER, *sees him still sitting on his chair against the back wall, and goes to get him, pushing and pulling him into position.* HUNTER *moves like a small child and sucks his thumb; when he is in position*) Ready?

SONYA   It's so hot inside.

BANNER   Follow me.

SONYA   I don't feel very well.

BANNER (*Irritated*)   Really! Some people!

SONYA (*To* ALAN)   I feel funny.
(BANNER *mimes knocking, calls out, and opens the door*)

BANNER (*Calls*)   The worshipers approach, god Arthur. All make reverence before thee.
(*They go in, much crowded together.* BANNER *motions them to kneel. They do so,* GERTRUDE *helping* HUNTER. *There is a great squash and much discomfort*)

LECTURER (*To the audience*)   There was some defect in the construction of the mask. It made the god sound as if he had no roof to his mouth. Mr. Banner, as priest of the god, supplied a running translation.

ARTHUR   Hee ha hee ho high.

BANNER   The god tells us we shall see great things.

GERTRUDE (*Whispers to* HUNTER) Great things.
(MURIEL *shushes her*)

ARTHUR Hi ha hay hahee ho hoo.

BANNER He has a surprise for us.

SONYA (*Whispers*) So *hot!*

BANNER Ssssh!

ALL Sssssh!

ALAN (*Whispers*) I'll take her out.

BANNER (*Whispers*) You will not.

ARTHUR Ha hee ha ha hi . . .

ALAN (*Whispers*) She's not well.

BANNER The god says . . .

ARTHUR (*Repeats*) Ha hee ha ha hi . . .
(SONYA *keels over in a faint. Silence. The others look
at her, and then, frightened, look at the god.* ARTHUR *looks
down at her*)

ARTHUR Ha hiracle.

BANNER A miracle.

ARTHUR Hee ha hee ho ho. Hy hee heahess ho he ho.

BANNER She has been overcome by the nearness of the god.

ALAN What should I do about it!

ARTHUR   Ha ee hou.

BANNER   Take her out.

ARTHUR   He hive he.

BANNER   Revive her.
(ALAN *looks around helplessly, then picks* SONYA *up in his arms and carries her out*)

MURIEL   Saucy! Putting herself forward.

GERTRUDE   Ssssh!

BANNER (*Motions* MURIEL *to bow her head again*)   Not if the god willed it, Mrs. Otterdale.
(*Looks at* ARTHUR *for confirmation*)

ARTHUR   Ha hee.

BANNER   He did.

ARTHUR   Hee hus hraie.

BANNER   Let us pray.
(*Silence from the upstairs area, as they pray.* ALAN *sets* SONYA *in the deck area. She holds him*)

ALAN   Are you O.K. eh, love? Are you?

SONYA   What's going to become of me?

ALAN   You'll be all right.

SONYA   The time's so near.

ALAN   I promise.

SONYA No doctor or nothing. Alan, I'm frightened.

ALAN We'll all help. I read a book. Natural birth—it's o.
ten done. Love, we'll all . . .

SONYA Bloody Children's Encyclopedia.

ALAN No, love. There's the women; they . . .

SONYA Not Muriel.
(*Pause*)

ALAN No. Not Muriel. I'll keep her away.
(*From the cabin area,* MURIEL *gives a scream, falls
down, froths, and rolls about.* ALAN *and* SONYA *hear
this and look, scared and puzzled, in that direction.
Overlapping dialogue follows:* ARTHUR *gives roofless
commands, which* BANNER *translates as "Remove her
. . . Loosen her clothing . . . She has been possessed . . ."* GERTRUDE *flaps—all this very quickly
and with more noise than dialogue.* BANNER *and*
TONY *carry* MURIEL *into the saloon area and lay her
out on the table*)

BANNER (*To* GERTRUDE) She has been possessed. You often hear of such cases in the United States. (BANNER
comes fussily out to SONYA *and* ALAN, *leaving the others
watching* MURIEL) Has she revived? She was possessed,
you know.

ALAN It was hot, that's all.

BANNER The holy spirit. It comes down and seizes them.
Muriel was possessed too. She fell down and foamed at
the mouth. It was most impressive.

91

ALAN   You shouldn't leave her, then.

BANNER   No I suppose not. Shall I bring Sonya some water?

SONYA   I'm all right now.

BANNER   What really worries me is the possibility that having been possessed, Muriel may bear fruit. (*Going*) You
must see how this undermines my position.
    (*A pause is broken by the* LECTURER)

LECTURER (*To the audience*)   I have used the words "the
god" so far because it seems that this is what Arthur sin-
cerely believed himself to be. But it was, as I've said, hot
in the holy place, and the air was offensive, and the circumstances uncomfortable. A god would not have minded
such matters. (*He has walked easily to the cabin area, and
stands behind* ARTHUR) But Arthur minded. There was a
small persistent voice inside that spoke to him. It was the
voice of his own doubt. As he grew more uncomfortable,
the voice became more insistent and more persuasive. I
speak now as the voice of Arthur's doubt. (*To* ARTHUR)
Can it be that you have made an elementary theological
error?

ARTHUR   Hee hoh.

LECTURER   Yes, it is hot. And horrid in every way. A god
could not be uncomfortable. But you are. Can it be that
you are not the god?

ARTHUR (*Reacts and moves away*)   Hi hah. Hi hah.

LECTURER   What if the god were only to inhabit you? Then
he could, at any time, leave. (*Pause*) No man could carry

the god within him forever. The god would not wish it. (*Pause*) Only for a time. To those found worthy. (*To the others*) Supper. November tenth.

BANNER (*Has an imaginary plate*)   I'll just take the god his first fruits, and be back directly.
> (BANNER *bears the plate to the cabin area, mimes knocking, enters with the imaginary plate which he makes a ceremony of laying at the god's feet*)

MURIEL   The god doesn't care for flying fish.

GERTRUDE   How do *you* know?

MURIEL   The god likes us to take trouble. We don't catch flying fish; they catch themselves. They fly on board during the night, and all we do is pick them up in the morning. You can't call that first fruits when there's no trouble in it.

GERTRUDE   You're not an authority on what the god likes.

MURIEL   Yes, I am.

GERTRUDE   Just because you say you've been possessed . . .

MURIEL   I have been possessed.

GERTRUDE   —that doesn't make you an authority.
> (BANNER *has returned*)

BANNER   Well, the god has been pleased to accept our little offering, and now we can all tuck in.

GERTRUDE   See? He does like flying fish.

MURIEL   He respects our feelings.

GERTRUDE   The god doesn't have to respect our feelings. We're supposed to respect him and his feelings. If he didn't like flying fish, he'd throw them back. Isn't that right, Harold?

BANNER   Well . . .

MURIEL   I don't pay any mind to you. You're jealous.

GERTRUDE   What have I got to be jealous about?

MURIEL   Because the god possessed me.

GERTRUDE   I was possessed a long time before you were, if you want to know. The god possessed me before he *was* a god.

ALAN   Gertrude, you never told us.

MURIEL   He was always a god. We didn't know it before.

GERTRUDE   Well, then?

MURIEL   Well then, what?

GERTRUDE   He was a god when he possessed me, then.

MURIEL   He never possessed you.

GERTRUDE   I know whether I was possessed or not.

BANNER   Ladies! Ladies!

MURIEL (*To* BANNER)   Shut up!!

94

BANNER Mrs. Otterdale!

MURIEL You're only the priest, but *I* was possessed.

GERTRUDE Why do you let her walk all over you, Harold?

MURIEL I don't pay any mind to you. Jealous bitch!

GERTRUDE Bitch! Did you call me a bitch?
(GERTRUDE *rises. She picks up an imaginary plate*)

LECTURER (*To* ARTHUR) The god stirs within you. You feel him uncoil within you.

MURIEL Bitch.

BANNER No. Don't throw anything. I'll tell the god.

GERTRUDE (*Shaking*) I've some pride left, Harold. I won't be insulted in front of everyone. I've had a lot of cruelty and inconsiderateness to put up with in my life, because I've always said what I thought and not pretended. I've sat alone in a tiny room—

MURIEL Bitch! Bitch!

GERTRUDE —waiting for the phone to ring. I've eaten dirt. I've been refused. I've watched my own pupils pretend not to see me in the foyers of theaters. I've been ignored in the street.

BANNER Now, Gertrude!

GERTRUDE What right has that woman to insult me? Tell me that. She falls down in a fit and calls it possession.

MURIEL That'll do from you. You keep your place. If the god prefers me to you, then you ought to take your medicine and keep quiet about it, instead of . . .

GERTRUDE Oh! You!
    (*She throws her imaginary plate.* MURIEL *dodges*)

LECTURER (*To* ARTHUR) He will go now. He will leave you now.
    (GERTRUDE *and* MURIEL *square up to each other, preparing to fight*)

BANNER Ladies!

ALAN Give over, Gertrude.

TONY I seen some lady wrestlers once. They had mud all over them.
    (MURIEL *launches an attack.* BANNER *flaps about, without actually touching them.* HUNTER *points his finger childishly at the two women, and begins to laugh*)

LECTURER (*To* ARTHUR) Now! (ARTHUR *gives a long scream. All activity in the saloon area stops dead. All look, shocked, toward the upstairs area. To* ARTHUR) He is going . . . going . . . He goes back. (ARTHUR *emits a continuous whimper*) He has gone.
    (ARTHUR *is still.* LECTURER *signals* ASSISTANTS, *who come to remove his mask*)

ALAN You'd better go and see what's happened.

BANNER I don't want to. I'm frightened.
    (ARTHUR *walks briskly into the saloon area. Silence.*

*He looks about him, at the women, and at the
imaginary plate)*

ARTHUR   Why are there broken plates upon the floor?
(*Pause. All look at each other*)

BANNER (*Timidly*)   Thy servants fought among themselves.

GERTRUDE (*A little bob*)   I'm sorry, god Arthur. The
woman provoked me, and I did throw a plate at her.

ARTHUR   I am not the god Arthur. The god Arthur has gone
back to heaven. I am his vicar here on earth. (*To* BANNER)
So you may remove that surplice, Mr. Banner. I shall be
the god's high priest from now on.
(*Pause*)

LECTURER (*To the cast*)   Evening service. (*All but* ARTHUR
bring chairs out to the deck area. HUNTER, *as always, is being guided and helped; they sit in two rows.* ARTHUR
*watches, waits until they are ready, then takes the ship's
log from the table, and comes out to them standing before
them as the priest.* LECTURER *speaks to the audience*)
They had a service every evening, out on the deck. It began with a reading from what had once been the ship's
log, then became the minutes of the New Society, and was
now the Book of Arthur.

ARTHUR (*Reads*)   There came a great wind over the surface
of the waters, and the waters rose up, and the face of the
sky was made black by the waters, and the voice of the god
Arthur was heard in the wind, crying, "Woe! Woe! to the
sons of men." Then many of those who were not of the

Selected were swallowed up. They and their wives, their children and their beasts, both of the greater and the lesser sort, were swallowed up. (ASSISTANT *makes a plopping noise with his mouth. Heads turn*) But over the Selected, the god held the shield of his hand, and all save one— being judged unworthy—were saved by the god.

TONY (*Quiet. To* SONYA) What one?

SONYA (*Whispers*) Wesley.

TONY Oh!
(ASSISTANT *makes a whole series of plops. Heads turn*)

BANNER High priest Arthur?

ARTHUR Yes?

BANNER May I be permitted to draw your attention to a natural phenomenon, doubtless sent to us by the god . . .
(ARTHUR *walks to the edge of the deck area, looking down into the front rows of the audience*)

ARTHUR Extraordinary! (*To the others*) The reading is over.

BANNER (*Timidly*) May we remain and observe the phenomenon?

ARTHUR Very well. We shall remain and await a sign.

LECTURER The night of the squid is confused in Armitage's account. At first there were only little squid, packed together in large numbers, covering the surface of the sea.

Our forefathers stayed on deck, watching. It became dark. And a little thread of wind came up to chill them.

SONYA Cold.

LECTURER Captain Hunter, what do you see?

HUNTER Lots of jolly little brown cobblestones. All over. You could walk to land if you knew where it was.

LECTURER No, after that. (HUNTER *begins to moan*) Muriel? Harold! Gertrude?

MURIEL Squiggly. Squiggly things.

BANNER Black.

GERTRUDE Snakes. Horrid black snakes.

LECTURER Touching. Exploring (*They all tilt*) Pulling.

MURIEL Nasty pulls us.

BANNER Demon.

ALAN Don't sit there. Hit them. Get them away.

ARTHUR He has laid his hand on the raft, and we feel the weight of it.

ALAN He?

LECTURER He. You see him. A squid. A giant squid . . . Two great tentacles and eight smaller ones, clustered about a giant head.

BANNER   Sea demon.

GERTRUDE   Horrid. Nasty snakes. Beaky things.

LECTURER   Pulling. Nearer and nearer.

ALAN   We could get indoors. Why don't we get indoors.

BANNER   High priest Arthur, pray, exorcise the demon before it eats us.

ARTHUR   My fate cries out.

LECTURER   Stop. It lets you go. (*To the audience*) The creature had tired of playing with the raft, and now disappeared.

GERTRUDE   (*Cries out*)   It's let us go.

ALAN   Pushed us away.

SONYA   It's gone. It's really gone.

HUNTER   (*Suddenly roars with laughter*)   Pushed us away! Old sea thing didn't want us, and pushed us away.
    (ARTHUR *has been still, apart from the others. Now he turns*)

ARTHUR   Be quiet.
    (*Pause*)

MURIEL   Arthur? You'll talk to the god? You won't let that sea thing come back?

BANNER   Of course he won't.

GERTRUDE   We must trust Arthur. He is all we have.

BANNER   And very powerful with the god.

MURIEL   You'll talk to him? I don't like that sea thing.
(*Pause*)

ARTHUR   Woman, that *was* the god. And he will come
again.
(*Pause*)

BANNER   The god?

ARTHUR   Yes. I had no power over him. You saw that.

BANNER   But what does he want?

ARTHUR   I cannot say. But he will come again.

ALAN   It was only a squid. You know that bloody well.
Frightening the women! It was a giant squid—that's all.

ARTHUR   The god can take many forms. He can take the
form of a man or a squid. But in any form, he is terrible.

ALAN   Oh, for Christ's sake, you don't really believe in all
that! (ARTHUR *steps forward and hits him. Then he turns
and goes inside to the cabin area, followed by* BANNER. *All
the others follow him inside except* SONYA *and* TONY, *who
sit on their chairs against the back wall.* SONYA *hesitates,
as if to stay with* ALAN) No. You go in. I'm in disgrace.
(SONYA *goes. An* ASSISTANT *comes to* ARTHUR *with a
frowning mask*) Bloody madness!

TONY   Oh, I dunno.

ALAN   You're not going in?

TONY Thought I might stay out here for a bit. I like watching the water. Relaxes you.

ARTHUR There is no place for blasphemers.

TONY (*Indicating the audience*) Funny—they've gone now. All them little squid. Well, they've not gone, I suppose! We've gone. Moved on past them. I often come out here and watch. Sonn and me, we . . .

ALAN Why don't you leave me alone?

ARTHUR Get him.
(*Pause.* BANNER *has left* ARTHUR *and comes onto the deck area*)

BANNER The high priest wants to see you in the temple. He's very angry. He says there's no place for blasphemers among the Selected. I'd make an act of contrition if I were you.

ALAN You think he'll have me thrown to the sharks?

BANNER I hope not.
(*Silence.* ALAN *stares at* BANNER)

ALAN But that was a joke.

BANNER An act of contrition should do it.

ALAN It was a *joke*. I mean, he couldn't really . . . You wouldn't let him. (*Silence*) I'll tell him I'm sorry.

BANNER It was a very evil and wicked remark.

ALAN Blasphemous. I see that. I'll tell him.

BANNER   He's waiting.
   (ALAN *walks in from the deck, stopping to give one wild and wondering glance to* BANNER, *who does not respond, but ushers him to the cabin area, where* ARTHUR *waits*)

TONY   (*As if speaking to the sharks*)   Well, I'm not going to be your dinner. I'll tell you that.

BANNER   The sinner approaches your presence, high priest.
   (*Goes back to his seat against the wall*)

ARTHUR   (*Turns away from the mask*)   Enter.
   (ALAN *enters*)

ALAN   I'm very sorry, high priest. I am truly sorry that I have sinned.

ARTHUR   The god is angry.

ALAN   I am truly . .

ARTHUR   I've told you before, sorrow is of no practical use without the intention of amendment.

ALAN   I do intend it.

ARTHUR   Well, it is necessary at the beginning that there should be one among the Selected to doubt and rebel.

ALAN   I'm not . . .

ARTHUR   . . . so that his chastisement by the god should be remembered by the people.

ALAN   I'm not rebelling, Arthur.

ARTHUR   Not at the moment. No.

ALAN   Never again.

ARTHUR   Well, you are not to be blamed for it. You do no less in your way than we all do in ours. You express the will of the god. He has willed your doubt, because he wills your expiation.

ALAN   What form would that take . . . Arthur?

ARTHUR   When the god came out of the sea just now, what did he want? It was not clear to me . . . I had thought foolishly that I was his only incarnation. Not true. Then he laid his hand on the raft, and I was powerless. It was the god himself.

ALAN   The god Arthur?

ARTHUR   In another form.

ALAN   It couldn't have been . . . an antigod?

ARTHUR   No, or I should have prevailed. It was the god himself—made squid.

ALAN   I should never have doubted it. I see that now.

ARTHUR   Then you spoke, I struck you, and I knew.

ALAN   What he wanted?

ARTHUR   Yes.

ALAN   And that is?

ARTHUR   Sacrifice. A sign of our belief. An offering.

ALAN (*Tentatively*)   We do sacrifice, high priest. We offer our first fruits to the god.

ARTHUR   That is an act of devotion, not a sacrifice. It does not hurt us to give them. Though . . . "first fruits" . . . Yes, even from the mouth of an unbeliever, the god may speak. First fruits . . . the god's appearance in the likeness of a sea creature . . . the delay in coming to land . . . Iphigenia . . . It all fits, Mr. Armitage. It is all of a piece.

ALAN   What . . . did you think of sacrificing, Arthur?

ARTHUR   What would you think most worthy?

ALAN   Not me. *I'm* not worthy. I—

ARTHUR   No.

ALAN   —though I'm ready, of course, to do as the god wills.

ARTHUR   Not you.
        (*Pause*)

ALAN   Later, perhaps.

ARTHUR   Perhaps.

ALAN   I don't know what you had in mind, of course—what the god had in mind . . . who . . .

ARTHUR   Why do you ask? It can make no difference. We are all equal in the eyes of the god.
        (*Pause*)

ALAN   It wouldn't be any of the women, of course . . . I mean, the god would want them to . . . to multiply . . . to

... (*Rattled*) there are some of the women it couldn't possibly be! There are some you—he'd want an unblemished body. A good body. Someone like Tony; he'd appreciate that. He'd want ... Or if you thought Harold ... If you thought he might relish Harold ...

ARTHUR The mechanics of the thing might need a little arrangement. That is often the case in matters of religion, is it not?

ALAN None of the women.

ARTHUR I shall need your help. Since you have a penance to perform, that is convenient.

ALAN The god wouldn't want a pregnant woman. It's taboo. That's the last person he'd want.
(*Pause*)

ARTHUR The pregnancy is much advanced.
(*Pause*)

ALAN I have to go to the lavatory.

ARTHUR No, you don't.
(*Pause*)

ARTHUR It would be better for the others not to know.

ALAN Eh?

ARTHUR A sacrifice need not be public to be effective. Only the will to give is important. Later on, the others would be told. That is the god's will.

ALAN But they'd notice. You couldn't ... It would cause grave resentment.

ARTHUR   The confinement will take place in the temple.

ALAN (*Desperately*)   I have a revelation from the god.

ARTHUR (*Carries straight on; the dialogue overlaps*)   We shall take the child.

ALAN   The child?

ARTHUR   An innocent life. Unblemished. For the god.

ALAN   The child?

ARTHUR   Yes.

ALAN   Not . . . ?

ARTHUR   Really, Mr. Armitage, have you been following me at all?

ALAN   You're going to take the child? . . . Oh . . . Oh yes, I had quite the wrong idea. Oh, that's wonderful. The child . . . Yes. Yes, you do: you must: that's much better. I was quite wrong. I was very afraid, and quite wrong. The child. (*Now it hits him*) But how can you tell her?

ARTHUR   There are anesthetics in the first-aid kit.

ALAN   You'll say it died in childbirth?

ARTHUR   It will be a secret we shall share with the god. Go now.
   (ALAN *begins to go, but hesitates*)

ALAN   There'll be . . . there'll be other children. It is best, isn't it? I mean, if *someone's* got to . . .

ARTHUR   The god demands it.

ALAN (*Going*)   Yes. I see that.
(*He goes into the saloon area. He is dazed.* SONYA *is sitting with the others against the back wall. He goes out on deck, ignores* TONY, *and sits on a corner of the deck, crouched in a back-to-the-womb position.* TONY *looks at him. Meanwhile, as he has left the main cabin,* SONYA *rises from her chair, looking after him*)

SONYA   Alan . . . (*She follows him out on deck*) Alan . . .

TONY   Over there.
(*She joins* TONY. *Pause. She takes a step toward* ALAN)

SONYA   Alan . . .

ALAN   Go away.

SONYA (*Small gesture to* TONY *to move away*)   What's the matter, love?

ALAN (*He hasn't looked around*)   I saw that.
(TONY *looks from one to another and hesitates*)

TONY   I'll go in, then.

ALAN   Why?
(*Pause*)

SONYA   Go on in, Tone.

ALAN   No.

SONYA (*To* TONY)   Go on in.

ALAN (*Shouts*)   I said, no.

TONY (*To* SONYA)   See you.

ALAN   You don't want to leave us alone, Tony. Nobody ever leaves Sonya and me alone. You're the only one who's ever alone with Sonya.

SONYA (*To* TONY)   Something's happened.

TONY   Arthur's given him a bollocking.

ALAN   Will you please stop talking *about* me? I'm not sick.

SONYA   Tell me what's happened, then.

ALAN   Just go away and leave me alone. Go away and do your exercises.

TONY (*To* SONYA)   What's he on about?

SONYA   Nothing. It's not important.

ALAN   Ha!

TONY   Stupid. You can't do exercises in the dark.

ALAN   Can't you?

SONYA   That's enough, Alan.

ALAN (*Turns to* TONY)   Tell me, Tony. Is Arthur god?

TONY   I don't follow you.

ALAN   Try. Just put one thought after another. It's a simple question. Is he a god? Do you obey him? Do you do his will?

SONYA   I said, that's enough.

ALAN   When you do your exercises, in the hold—do you glory in it? A religious act?

TONY   I don't know what you're on about. It's nothing to do with me, all that about religion. I just keep out of trouble. (*Pause.* ALAN *gets up*)

ALAN   You smug bastard! Arthur, and what he does to us— that's none of your business.

SONYA   Tony, go inside.

ALAN   What he does to us, and what he makes us do—you don't want to know. We can destroy ourselves, and as long as you do your bloody exercises down in the hold, it doesn't matter.

SONYA   What do you mean. "What he *makes* us do"?

ALAN   Do you think I don't know what sort of exercises you get up to?

SONYA (*Loses her temper*)   No, you don't. You don't know any bloody thing. (*Pause*)

TONY (*Puzzled, to* SONYA)   But it's not like that.

SONYA   He's jealous.

TONY You never told him we . . .

ALAN She wouldn't tell me you didn't.

TONY (*To* SONYA) Why not?

SONYA He wouldn't have believed me. He won't believe
you now.
(*Pause*)

TONY (*To* ALAN) You stupid bastard. You don't know
nothing about it. (*Pause*) I can't, if you want to know.
(*Pause*) It's not that I don't fancy you, Sonn, I do, as a
matter of fact.

SONYA Tony, this is not the time.

TONY But I just can't; that's all. I don't know why. If it was
anyone else, it'd be funny. Laughable. When I was six-
teen, the boys used to call me a sex maniac—I wore myself
out; it wasn't healthy. Then I saw an ad in the papers,
Why be a ninety-eight-pound weakling. And I wanted to
look good on the beach and that, and I thought doing exercises might take me mind off it, you know what I mean.
And after a bit I found I wasn't interested no more. I
thought it was the exercise done it. Being tired when I
come home from the gym. And then I won all them prizes,
and had me picture on the cover of *Health and Strength,*
and they was all after me—I could take me pick—and
then when I did want to, I just couldn't.

SONYA Tony! Give over. Give over, eh?

TONY I've tried. There was one bird I fancied, she wouldn't
believe it. She thought I was queer, and she could cure me,

but I'm not. (*Pause*) So now you know. She's safe with
me. Any bird's safe with me.
(*Pause*)

ALAN   I'm sorry.
(SONYA *comes over to* TONY *and kisses him*)

ALAN   Jealousy! You imagine things. You get sick with it.

SONYA   Sick!

ALAN   I've been stupid.

SONYA   You think nobody in the world exists but you.
You're sick, and we've all got to die of it.

ALAN   Sonn, we've got to get away from here.

SONYA   Why? So that you can have me all to yourself again?
I'll tell you now it won't work. First thing you know,
you'll be saying, "Who are you thinking about? Who did
you dream about last night? Who do you think of when
you kiss me?" I tell you, Alan Armitage, *I'm* the one who's
sick, and it's time you remembered. I'm really sick. I get
sick in the mornings. I throw up. I get so frightened, I'm
sick. And I'm sick to death of you.

ALAN (*To* TONY)   Tony, will *you* help us? He won't know.
He won't know you helped. (*Pause*) Or you can come
with us, if you like. He can come with us, Sonn.
(*Pause*)

TONY   He give you more than a bollocking.

SONYA   What did he say to you in there?

ALAN   He says the god needs a sacrifice. He says that's why it came out of the sea. He says it wants a life—something new and innocent. He says when the baby is born, I have to help him sacrifice it to the god.

TONY   And you said?

ALAN   I was frightened. There was nobody to help me. What could I say?

TONY   What did you say?

ALAN   I said I would.

TONY   You must be bloody mad. (TONY *walks straight into* ARTHUR's *room, miming throwing open the door*) You! (ARTHUR *begins to rise.* LECTURER *stops him*)

LECTURER   Wait! The god protects you. He possesses you. (ARTHUR *begins to put on the mask.* TONY *grabs it and throws it aside*)

TONY   Bloody kids' stuff.
(ASSISTANT *gives* ARTHUR *a piece of wood shaped like a knife.* ARTHUR *stabs* TONY, *who cries out.* ARTHUR *escapes into saloon area*)

ARTHUR   Stop him! He is attacking the god.
(TONY *follows* ARTHUR, *clasping his shoulders. The other characters leave their places and come into the saloon. They watch*)

TONY   This loony wants to kill little kids.

ARTHUR   Mr. Armitage, you had no business to speak of this. Pray do your duty, and protect me.

TONY   You keep out of this. Bastard pulled a knife on me.
I'll fix him.

ARTHUR   You will be helpless without me.

BANNER   No one must interfere. It is for the god himself to
settle.
(TONY *and* ARTHUR *circle the table. But suddenly*
ARTHUR *stops. It must appear as if the actor himself
has forgotten his lines and has begun to feel ill. He
leaves the fight and supports himself by first holding
onto, then sitting on the table*)

ARTHUR   Sorry. I can't go on.
(*The cast are surprised. They look at the* LECTURER
*for guidance. They will remain still until their next
move is indicated, and will always be looking at the*
LECTURER, *wherever he may be*)

LECTURER   What?

ARTHUR   I can't go on. I know what will happen.

LECTURER   You are Arthur. You know only what he knows.
You cannot know the future.

ARTHUR   I know what will happen. I was a student here.
(LECTURER *signals to* ASSISTANT, *who goes offstage*)

LECTURER (*Gentle*)   If you know that, if you can remember that, then you know that you will survive it, and go
free afterward.

ARTHUR   But Arthur will die. Tony will break his neck.
And I will feel his death. His pain. And you make this
happen. You make me Arthur.

LECTURER   You volunteered.

ARTHUR   Yes, I volunteered for prison too, do you remember? We all volunteer. (*To the audience*) You volunteered to attend this lecture. You volunteered to be students, and those who are not students, volunteered not to be. We volunteer to obey in this community. We . . .

LECTURER   Stop! (ASSISTANT *has brought him a small glittering object, probably a revolving mirror set against a reflector. He holds it up, compelling* ARTHUR *to watch*) Now let me help you. Look at me. Watch. Watch now. Submit now. Give me your will so that I can help you. You want to obey because you are part of us. The community wills it. You are the god Arthur, and you must die for us all. You are the god, Arthur. You know that now. You are the god.
(*Pause.* LECTURER *appears satisfied and returns to his place*)

ARTHUR   No. I don't think so.

LECTURER   What?

ARTHUR   You are the god.

LECTURER   I am Leading Lecturer in the History of the Community; that is all. And you are Arthur Henderson. The god Arthur.

ARTHUR   There are no gods but you. You are the resurrection and the life. You put us here. You plan out the path we are to travel. But I have free will, and I choose not to die, so you can keep your resurrection.

LECTURER   You choose to be what you are—Arthur Henderson. When this is over, you will be . . .

ARTHUR   Reborn? But what if I choose to be Arthur in my own way? If I choose to change your history? To be Arthur, and kill Tony?

LECTURER   If you defy me, you will not kill Tony. He is stronger than you are and will break your neck just the same. If you choose to fight him in defiance, as your own sick self, instead of in obedience as Arthur Henderson, a person in history, I cannot revive you. But if you submit to me, though you will suffer pain—and you want to suffer it, that is part of your cure—yet you will be revived as Wesley was. Now! (*He raises his hand*) Look at me. I will snap my fingers, and . . .

ARTHUR   No. I am myself. I will overcome.

LECTURER   Very well, Mr. Batch—continue. (ARTHUR *turns and rushes at* TONY. *They fight.* ARTHUR *drops the knife.* TONY *gets a grip round* ARTHUR's *neck and is clearly about to kill him*) Wait! (*All freeze. But* ARTHUR, *though he cannot move, being held in* TONY's *grip, is not hypnotized. The* LECTURER *speaks to* ARTHUR) You see? (AR-THUR *is humiliated and does not reply*) Think yourself lucky that the community cares even for its disobedient members, or I should not have saved you. (*To the audience*) We shall not carry this scene to its conclusion, for reasons that must be obvious to you. However, you may take it that the course of history was not changed. Tony killed Arthur, and with the death of the god they came to land, and our New Society began. I do not wish

116

you to undervalue Arthur Henderson. Those early minutes of the New Society are the source of many of
our community rules. Our very first community leader
was, in fact, the son whom Muriel Otterdale bore to Arthur after his death. The community always uses what is
good in a man. Next week we shall discuss the Early
Settlement, the Period of Chaos, and the Evolution of the
Community Spirit. Mr. Batch, remain. Places, you others.
(ALAN, SONYA, HUNTER, BANNER, *and* MURIEL *return to
their places.* LECTURER *goes to where* TONY *still holds* AR-
THUR, *using* ARTHUR *as a specimen in his talk to the audience*) In the case of this criminal who presented Arthur
to you, you have been able to study the effects of advanced
individualism, which made him as we now discover, a bad
subject for hypnosis, and has caused us technical difficul-
ties during the lecture. However, the community does not
and will not allow waste of any kind. We cure criminals;
we do not kill them. This man will be returned to medical
care—

ARTHUR   No.

LECTURER (*Ignores him*) —and you may be sure that,
however long it takes, however intense the treatment, in
the end he will walk among us again, a free and obedient
member of the community.

LECTURER Mr. Batch!—

ARTHUR (*Interrupts*)   Kill the god!
        (*He clicks his fingers as the* LECTURER *has done.*
        TONY *acts automatically, tightening his grip.* LEC-
        TURER *is caught by surprise and is just too late*)

117

LECTURER Release him! (TONY *releases* ARTHUR *but it is too late. He drops to the ground, dead.* ASSISTANT *kneels to examine him, but* LECTURER *crosses quickly, waves* ASSISTANT *away, then kneels to examine the body himself. Then he orders the* ASSISTANTS) Remove the prisoners.
(ASSISTANT *touches* TONY *and motions him offstage. He goes.* ASSISTANTS *go to the other prisoners, touching each, and indicating the way offstage.* BANNER *and* MURIEL *are last on opposite sides. When* BANNER *is touched*)

BANNER We have come to land, Muriel.

MURIEL I wonder how we shall go on there, then.
(LECTURER *stands to address the audience*)

LECTURER This prisoner is dead.

MURIEL I wonder how we shall go on there, then.

LECTURER I have told you this was no part of the intention of the lecture. Consequently it is clear that the man himself chose . . . that the man chose his own death. (*Crossing to the lectern to gather up his notes*) There will be no questions.

MURIEL (*Heard from offstage*) I wonder how we shall go on there, then.

LECTURER (*Begins to leave the stage*) You will not discuss what has happened.
(*He goes. We hear* MURIEL'*s voice once more, as left, spotlit, where it has fallen*)

MURIEL I wonder how we shall go on there, then.

Curtain